MAKING
HOMEMADE
SOUPS & STEWS

MAKING
HOMEMADE
SOUPS & STEWS

PHYLLIS HOBSON

Illustrated by Elayne Sears

GARDEN WAY PUBLISHING
CHARLOTTE, VERMONT 05445

Line drawings by Elayne Sears

Printed in the United States by Capital City Press,
Third Printing, March 1980

Library of Congress Cataloging in Publication Data

Hobson, Phyllis.
  Making homemade soups & stews.

  Includes index.
  1. Soups.   2. Stews.   I. Title.
TX757.H58   641.8'13   77–17025
ISBN 0–88266–110–8 pbk.

Contents

Introduction

Homemade soup has been called a soother of nerves, a starter of digestive juices. It is, but a good homemade soup is much more.

The aroma of a kettle of soup simmering on the back of the stove can fill a house with warmth. It can say "welcome" to returning members of the family.

The taste of hot soup can be comforting on a cold day. Chilled, it can be refreshing on a hot summer afternoon.

Soup or stew can be a convenience to the busy cook who can tend to the soup or stew pot while she goes about her tasks. It can be made in the evening, refrigerated and saved for a day or two, then served on one of those days when there are errands to be run, or meetings to attend and no time to prepare a meal.

Homemade soup and stew can mean better nutrition for the vegetable snubbers in the family or for children and the elderly who find it difficult to chew the tougher cuts of meat. Not only are the meats and vegetables in bite-size pieces in soups, but much of their nutrients are in the liquid—the vitamin, mineral, calcium-rich soup broth.

And homemade soup and stew can be a delicious way to save money, to make better use of the foods we buy and grow and process. Because it uses foods which might otherwise be discarded, soup can help us make a more complete use of food supplies in these times of inflation and shortages.

But there is yet another reason for making soup and stew.

All of us search for fulfillment in work and hobbies. We like to create, to use our imaginations. What better way to feel fulfilled than to start with a few scraps of food—a bone, a few leftover vegetables, some herbs and a little imagination—and create a delicate broth or a one-dish meal that satisfies the appetite and nourishes the body.

Making soup and stew can be challenging, imaginative, creative. It can be fun.

Soup Can Save You Money

Would you like to serve your family at least one delicious meal a week almost free of charge? You can if it is homemade soup.

Here's how it works: Let's say you have tucked away in your refrigerator the bones and a couple of leftover wings from last Sunday's roast chicken, one serving of peas, a dab of lima beans and four spears of cooked asparagus, all of which will be thrown out at the end of the week.

You also have a limp rib of celery and three small, tired carrots. Back in the corner you have a few cups of accumulated vegetable cooking water which would have gone down the drain if you hadn't saved it. In the cabinet you have half a cup of commercial noodles.

It doesn't sound like much of a meal, does it? It can be, and here's how:

LEFTOVER SOUP

Leftover carcass from roast chicken
2 quarts water
1 teaspoon salt
1 quart accumulated vegetable cooking water
1 rib celery, sliced
3 small carrots, sliced
1/2 cup peas
1/4 cup cooked lima beans
4 spears cooked asparagus, sliced
1/2 cup commercial noodles
Salt and pepper

3

Break up chicken bones and simmer two hours in the water in which the salt has been added. Drain broth into soup kettle and set bones aside to cool. Add vegetable cooking water, celery and carrots to broth. Simmer 15 minutes. Add peas, lima beans, asparagus, noodles and chicken meat picked from bones. Simmer 15 minutes more. Season to taste with salt and pepper. Makes about 2 quarts of soup.

By serving a delicious, nutritious homemade soup like this for lunch and for dinner at least one night a week, you can trim several dollars off your weekly food budget. If your time is limited during the week, serve soup for Saturday lunch and Sunday night supper or make the soup when you have more time on the weekends and refrigerate it for Monday or Tuesday night's dinner.

But don't get into a rut on the types of soup you make. Aim for a variety of meats and vegetables, of textures and thicknesses. Try to prepare a new soup each week.

Use the recipes in this book not as strict formulas to be followed exactly, but as guidelines to be improved upon and embellished. Use your imagination as well as the foods you have on hand. If the recipe calls for carrots, try rutabagas or peas. If you have no meat stock, substitute bouillon cubes and water. Try tomato juice in place of milk.

Use your judgment, too, in amounts of the ingredients. If a soup is too thick, add water or stock. If it seems too thin, add less. If your family is fond of onion, you may want to double the amounts in the recipe.

For the cook's convenience, the ingredients in each recipe are listed in the order used. Because the size of a serving may vary greatly according to the size of the soup bowl, the type of soup or peoples' appetites, the quantity of each recipe is given in quarts rather than servings. (You may estimate 1 to 1^1/$_2$ cups per serving.) These quantities are approximate, too, because the amount of liquid may vary with the length and temperature of cooking.

For larger families, or to prepare large batches for canning and freezing, all of the recipes may be doubled or even tripled. For smaller families, they may be halved.

To make serving—and eating—soup more interesting, collect a repertoire of soup dishes that add eye appeal to your meals. Make your soups more tempting by serving bouillon in crystal cups or consomme in elegant China soup plates. Serve gumbo in colorful pottery bowls and cream soups in thick crockery mugs. And for real elegance, treat your dinner guests to soup served from Grandmother's beautiful old soup tureen.

Equipment You'll Need

The Soup Kettle—Once you have acquired the happy habit of serving soup once or twice a week, you will want to beg or buy a soup kettle. You may need two if you plan to make it in large quantities.

For one or two-meal quantities of soup, an 8 to 10-quart stainless steel kettle is ideal. It will hold all ingredients, yet can be stored easily in the refrigerator. For making larger quantities, a hot water bath canner or a 16-quart steam pressure canner is convenient and thrifty, since it can serve double use in canning as well as making the soup.

Colander or Food Mill—Many of the following recipes contain the instructions: "Force through a colander or food mill." In order to extract the pulp of vegetables and remove the tougher portions (such as celery strings and bean hulls) and remove large herb pieces, you'll need a colander (with or without a wooden pestle) or a food mill of some kind. There are many types available, ranging from the simple cranked mill to more elaborate juicer-presses.

Collecting Ingredients

Think "soup" all during the week as you prepare your meals. Almost any meat or vegetable can provide an ingredient for the soup kettle and thus never should be discarded unless it is spoiled or rancid.

Save the cooking water and the canning liquids from all vegetables and keep them refrigerated until soup-making time.

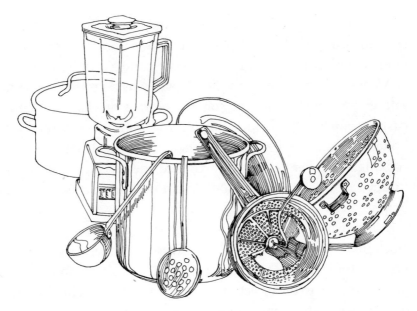

Rinse out roasting pans after cooking meats and poultry, pour this broth into a container and refrigerate. Don't worry about removing the fat. It will solidify and can be lifted off the top later.

And don't forget the vitamin-rich water left after blanching garden vegetables for the freezer. A quart or two of spinach or asparagus water can add a new dimension to vegetable-beef soup.

Learn to scrub vegetables well before peeling and then save all the parings (from potatoes, carrots, turnips, rutabagas), the trimmed parts of asparagus and radishes, celery leaves and the tops of green onions. Add them to your soup kettle for good nutrition and good taste, and at no cost.

Keep a plastic bag in the vegetable crisper of the refrigerator, in which to store all these vegetable scraps and peelings and any vegetables past their prime. Label and date all leftovers and use within a week.

On soup-making day, all these otherwise useless ingredients

can be combined in the soup kettle. Add a soup bone or two, a few herbs if you like, and cover all with water. Simmer 3 or 4 hours over low heat, strain off the broth and season to taste.

Meat stock can be made at little cost by using soup bones for sale at the supermarket or sometimes free of charge from a custom butcher. (Tell him they're dog bones if you're shy.) Bones also may be cut from roasts and steaks at home before cooking. Leftover bones from cooked meats or a chicken or turkey carcass can be used, too. And don't forget to ask for the bones when you have a beef or a calf butchered.

Whenever you get a supply of bones, make a batch of meat stock in your large soup kettle or pressure canner. If you have no need for stock at the time, or if you make a lot, can the surplus according to the directions on page 15 or pour it into plastic or glass containers and store it in the freezer.

Many of the recipes in this book call for vegetables to be cooked and then discarded when the broth is strained off. You can use them too, however. Chop them fine or run them through the blender before cooking and leave them in the soup. Most of the vitamins, however, are extracted from the vegetables in the long, slow cooking of the broth and few nutrients are left in the cooked vegetables.

Straining of the broth, also, permits you to use those vegetables which might otherwise be wasted, such as the tough ends of asparagus, wilted celery ribs, scraps and parings—which contain good nutrition and flavor, too.

Soup For Breakfast?

Of course you know that clear bouillon is a delicious appetizer for dinner, that a hearty vegetable-meat soup is a meal in itself.

And almost everyone has served thrifty bean soups or nourishing cream soups for lunch or Sunday night supper. You may even have whipped up a few bowlsful of French onion soup or a cream of vegetable soup for late night snacks.

But have you ever tried soup for breakfast?

Nutritionally, homemade soup makes a much better breakfast than the traditional bacon and eggs (both of which are high in cholesterol), or ready-made cereals, which are high in calories and low in protein and vitamins. It's even better for you than hot cooked cereals such as oatmeal, which supplies more starch than protein.

Homemade soup tastes good the first thing in the morning, while it fulfills the requirements of a good breakfast better than almost anything else. It can provide one-third of the day's needed supply of protein, vitamins, minerals and calcium. What's more, it can provide them at low cost in convenient, quick-fix form. A bowl or two of soup can be taken in the morning from the refrigerator and heated in less time than it takes to cook oatmeal or fry bacon and eggs, and at far less cost.

Making Soups and Stews with Home Appliances

Although soups often are cooked for long periods, they require far less energy to prepare than many other foods because they are simmered at low temperatures.

However, you can prepare them and consume even less energy by using several household appliances you may have on hand:

Blender—Many of the soup recipes call for chopping vegetables, cooking them and then forcing the vegetables through a colander or food mill. Most of these vegetables may be quickly run through the blender until finely chopped—to speed the cooking process. Or they may be puréed after cooking by liquifying them in the blender. The exceptions are tough or stringy vegetables, such as celery or asparagus, whose fibers sometimes will survive even blender blades.

Pressure Pan or Cooker—Although a higher heat is used, soups can be prepared quickly in a pressure cooker, thus saving some heat and time. This appliance is especially useful in making stock from bones, because it extracts the calcium and minerals more efficiently.

To make soup in a pressure pan or cooker, prepare the stock according to the recipe, being sure the cooker or canner is no more than half full. Bring the gauge to 15 pounds pressure, according to the manufacturer's directions. Lower heat and cook 25 minutes at that pressure. Turn off heat and leave undisturbed until the pressure returns to zero, then remove lid and strain off broth.

Clean out the pressure pan or cooker, picking off any meat from the bones. Discard bones and cooked herbs and vegetables. Return broth and meat to the pressure pan and follow remaining recipe directions, covering the pressure pan with an ordinary pan lid.

Slow Cooker—If you've enjoyed the convenience and good flavor a "Crock Pot" can provide, you'll want to use it often for making soups, since most of the recipes in this book may be made in one. Those which are not suitable are the cream soups and those soups which require a larger-capacity kettle. To speed the cooking time, heat the soup to simmering on the stove before adding to the cooker or, if your cooker is adjustable, first set the dial on high, then lower the temperature for the long, slow cooking that gives the food its distinctive good taste.

Stove Oven—When you plan to have your oven hot for long periods, such as when you cook a roast, for instance, plan also to make soup (with bones cut from the roast). Just bring the soup liquid to boiling, cover the kettle and place it in the oven with the roast. As long as the oven is hot, the soup will simmer. No stirring is necessary and there's no extra charge for the cooking.

Electric Skillet—Many soups may be prepared conveniently in an electric skillet or saucepan, which may use less energy than the top of the gas or electric range. Follow the manufacturer's directions and the recipe. Set the dial on low when liquid begins to simmer.

Wood Stove—The most efficient energy saver of all may be a wood-burning stove. If you are the proud owner of an old-fashioned cookstove, you probably already know how delicious home-made soups can be when simmered slowly at the back of the stove where the heat is low. And it's just as good and economical when simmered on the back of a wood-burning heating stove.

Canning and Freezing

Where homemade soups and stew are concerned, there is a way to have your cake and eat it too. The "cake" in this case is the convenience, economy and good flavor that comes from making soups and stews in large quantities.

The method is simple: Go ahead and make a full soup kettle of soup; then can or freeze the surplus. Better still, when the garden is bursting at the seams or when you have a large supply of bones or an unexpected amount of spare time, double or triple the amount of the soup recipe; then store it for use on those days when you have no time to prepare a hot lunch or a hearty, healthful dinner.

Freezing Soups and Stews

The following categories of stews and soups may be frozen successfully by completing the recipe, cooling and then freezing and storing it in pint or quart containers at zero degrees:

Clear Soups
Main Dish Soups (except Beef-Dumpling Soup)
Meal-in-One-Bowl Soups
Bean Soups (except Cream of Bean Soup)
Vegetable Soups
Fish and Shellfish Soups

Chowders
Gumbos
Chili Soups
Stews

Not suitable for freezing are cream soups or any soup in which milk or potatoes are main ingredients. Milk tends to curdle when thawed and potatoes become grainy.

To serve frozen soup or stew, thaw, then reheat, or reheat over hot water without thawing. It is best to season soups after reheating, since salted foods tend to turn rancid faster in freezing and pepper loses its flavor.

Canning Soups and Stews

Most stews and soups may be canned except cream soups and those which contain cabbage or any of the cole vegetables (broccoli, Brussels sprouts, kohlrabi, cauliflower, etc.) Because these vegetables tend to become strong flavored when canned, it is best to freeze soups and stews containing them or to add the vegetable just before serving.

Recipes which call for milk or thickening should be canned without these ingredients, which may be added just before serving.

Recipe categories in this book which are suitable for canning include:

Clear Soups
Main Dish Soups (except Beef-Dumpling Soup)
Meal-in-One-Bowl Soups (except French Pot-au-Feu, Hotch
    Potch and Russian Cabbage soups)

Bean Soups (except Cream of Bean Soup)
Vegetable Soups (except Cabbage and Vegetarian Vegetable)
Fish and Shellfish Soups
Chowders
Gumbos
Chili Soups
Stews (execpt Cheese Stew and Hungarian Stew)

Any soup or stew which contains even *one* low acid vegetable must be canned in a steam pressure canner. This includes all the recipes in this book except the recipe for Tomato Soup on page 73. If it is made with high-acid tomatoes (which may be canned safely by the hot water method) that one recipe alone may be canned as shown below. If it is made with the newer, low-acid tomatoes, you will need to add $1/2$ teaspoon citric acid or 2 tablespoons white distilled vinegar to the recipe on page 73 before proceeding as follows:

Follow recipe to completion. Pour hot soup into pint or quart hot canning jars to within $1/2$ inch of the top of the jar.

Wipe top and threads of jar with clean cloth and put on cap which has been rinsed in boiling water. As it is filled, place each jar on rack in empty hot water bath canner. When all jars are filled, pour hot water over them, filling the canner with water at least one inch over the top of the jars. Cover and bring water to a boil. Reduce heat slightly and keep just at boiling 45 minutes for pints, 1 hour for quarts.

To can all other soups and stews, follow the recipe through the preparation of the broth to the addition of the vegetables. Do not cook vegetables which will remain in soup or stew and leave out any milk or flour called for. Combine uncooked vegetables well with other ingredients and fill canning jars to within 2 inches of top of jar. Add water to within 1 inch of top. Adjust caps. Follow directions for use according to the manufacturer of your *pressure canner* and process pints 1 hour and quarts 1 hour, 30 minutes at 10 pounds pressure (240 degrees).

Soup Stocks

Flavorful soup stock is a delicious light soup for invalids and as the first course for a formal meal. It is ideal, too, as a low-calorie snack for dieters. Serve it piping hot in cold weather; chilled and jellied in summer.

Soup stock also is a basic ingredient for making many other soups and stews, and many of the recipes in this book call for stocks and broths. Although a specific stock may be called for, they often may be used interchangeably, or broths made from a variety of meats and vegetables may be used.

Soup stocks add a great deal of flavor and nutrition when used instead of water as the liquid in gravies, stews and casseroles, in cooking rice or noodles and when substituted for part of the milk in cream sauces for meats and vegetables.

Because many of the nutrients in the meats and vegetables leach into the liquid during the long, slow cooking, stocks and broths are rich in minerals and heat-stable vitamins. Be sure to include bones—broken and cracked as much as possible—in your soup kettle, too. Bones can add valuable calcium to your diet. Make use of your pressure cooker as outlined on page 10, or cook in soup kettle according to the recipes.

Use the following recipes as guidelines for making soup stocks. For flavor, use a variety of meats, bones and vegetables. For economy, use those ingredients available at least cost.

BROWN STOCK

1 pound lean beef, cut in small cubes	2 carrots, sliced
	1 turnip, chopped
2 tablespoons cooking oil	10 peppercorns
5 pounds beef bones	6 whole cloves
5 quarts cold water	1 bay leaf
1 medium onion, chopped	3 sprigs parsley
4 ribs celery, chopped	Salt

Brown beef over medium heat in cooking oil. Put browned meat cubes and bones in soup kettle and add cold water. Let stand 1 hour to draw out the juices, then add remaining ingredients. Cover and simmer 3 to 4 hours. Strain stock into shallow pan and chill overnight in refrigerator. Meanwhile, pick out pieces of meat and discard bones, cooked vegetables and herbs. Meat cubes may be used for other dishes. When chilled, lift hardened fat off the top of the stock. Makes 3 quarts Brown Stock.

WHITE STOCK

3 pounds knuckle veal	1/2 teaspoon peppercorns
1 pound lean beef or veal	1 bay leaf
3 quarts cold water	2 sprigs thyme
1 onion, chopped	2 whole cloves
1 carrot, sliced	Salt and pepper
1 rib celery, sliced	

Remove any meat from veal knuckle and cut into small pieces. Cut beef or veal in small pieces. Place bone and meat in soup kettle. Add cold water and let it stand 1 hour to draw out the juices. Slowly bring to the simmering point. Skim and add

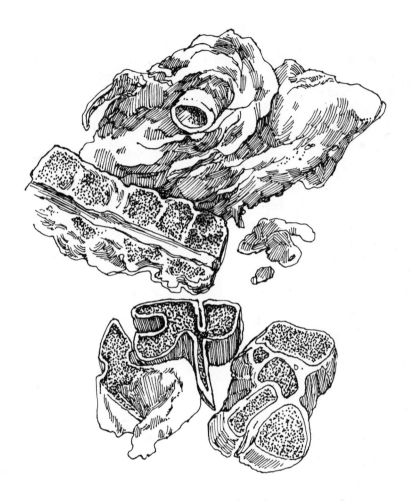

vegetables. Cover and simmer over low heat 3 to 4 hours. Tie peppercorns, bay leaf, thyme and cloves in a piece of cheese-cloth. Add to soup kettle. Cook 30 minutes longer. Remove cheesecloth bag and discard. Lift out bone and discard. Strain stock through three thicknesses of cheesecloth and chill to congeal fat. Lift off hardened fat and re-heat. Season to taste with salt and pepper. Pieces of meat may be used in meat dishes. Makes 2 quarts White Stock.

FISH STOCK

4 pounds white-fleshed fish, with bones	1/2 cup chopped parsley
10 cups cold water	2 garlic cloves, minced
1/2 cup chopped onion	2 whole cloves
1/2 cup chopped celery	Salt and pepper
1/2 cup chopped carrot	1/2 teaspoon dried thyme

Put all ingredients in soup kettle except thyme. Let stand 1 hour to draw out the juices. Cover and simmer 2^{1}/$_{2}$ hours. Add the thyme and simmer 15 minutes more. Cool and strain. Salt and pepper to taste. Makes 2 quarts Fish Stock.

To Clarify Soup Stock:

To each quart of cold soup stock, add one slightly beaten egg white and the egg shell, crushed with the hand. Heat, stirring constantly, until the stock boils. Let boil vigorously 5 minutes, then add ^{1}/$_{2}$ cup cold water for each quart of stock. Remove from heat. Let stand 5 minutes. Strain through three thicknesses of cheesecloth.

To Remove Fat from Stock:

Because greasy soup is high in cholesterol and calories as well as distasteful, remove as much as possible of the animal fat from the soup stock. To do this, yet make use of the less expensive, fatty meats, you can remove every trace of fat with this simple method:

When stock is finished cooking, strain off into a shallow pan. Refrigerate overnight or for several hours. When it is thoroughly chilled, the fat will have risen to the top and solidified. You can then lift off the hardened fat and discard it (or save it for making soap). Remove any bits of fat on the surface of the stock by wiping it with a dampened paper towel.

Making Clear Soups

The clear soups—bouillons, broths, consommés and madrilenes —contain the essence of the meats and vegetables from which they are made. They offer good nutrition with fewer calories because they contain only the cooking liquid into which the vitamins and minerals have leached.

The clear soups in this section are delicious in their own right, but many of them also may be used as bases for some of the heartier soups which follow.

Bouillons

Bouillons are clear soups made from lean meats or vegetables delicately seasoned. They often are used in combination with other soups, as in Tomato Bouillon.

Bouillons are simple soups, so serve them simply with sandwiches, in bouillon cups, or as the one hot dish with summer salad meals.

BEEF BOUILLON

6 pounds lean beef, cut up	2 tablespoons butter or
1 pound bones, cracked	margarine
3 quarts cold water	1 small whole onion
1/4 cup celery, diced	6 whole cloves
1/4 cup carrot, chopped	6 peppercorns
1 teaspoon green pepper, finely chopped	Salt

Cover meat and bones with cold water. Let stand 1 hour to draw
out juices. Bring slowly to simmering and cook 4 hours over low
heat. Meanwhile, in a small skillet, sauté celery, carrot and
green pepper in butter or margarine until lightly browned. Add
to meat stock. Stud onion with cloves. Add onion and peppercorns. Cook one hour longer. Strain and season to taste with
salt. Cool, remove hardened fat and clarify (page 20). Makes
2 quarts Bouillon.

TOMATO BOUILLON

2 cups puréed fresh or
  canned tomatoes
1 teaspoon sugar
1 teaspoon onion juice

1/4 teaspoon celery salt
2 cups Beef Bouillon
Salt and pepper
Parsley

Purée tomatoes by running through blender or forcing through a colander or food mill. Over low heat, bring the tomato pulp to a boil. Add sugar, onion juice, celery salt and Beef Bouillon. Let simmer 10 minutes to blend flavors. Season to taste with salt and pepper. Serve in cups garnished with finely chopped parsley. Makes 1 quart bouillon.

VEGETABLE BOUILLON

2 tablespoons sugar
1 medium onion, chopped
1 carrot, chopped
3 ribs celery, chopped
2 quarts cold water
1 head lettuce, shredded
2 whole cloves

4 medium tomatoes, chopped
  (or 2 cups canned tomatoes)
1 bay leaf
1 blade (or 1/2 tsp. ground)
  of mace
Salt and pepper

In a heavy skillet, brown the sugar, then add the onion and stir until the onion is browned. Add the chopped carrot and celery and the cold water. Stir well. Add remaining ingredients and bring slowly to simmering. Cook gently 2 hours. Strain, then clarify according to directions on page 20. Season to taste with salt and pepper. Makes 2¹/₂ quarts Bouillon.

Broths

Broths are mildly flavored clear soups made with almost any meat or combination of meats.

Most of the following broths are flavored with a small amount of vegetables, but simple broths may be made by simmering the meat in water until the juices are extracted, then straining off the broth and seasoning it lightly with salt and pepper.

The cooked meat may be used for casseroles or other meat dishes. The broths are used as simple soups or as a base for other soups.

BEEF BROTH

Sprig thyme	2 quarts cold water
Sprig parsley	1 carrot, chopped
Sprig marjoram	1 turnip, chopped
12 peppercorns	2 ribs celery, chopped
2 pounds uncooked bones, with meat scraps	1 onion, chopped
	Salt

Tie thyme, parsley, marjoram and peppercorns in a piece of cheesecloth. Place bones in soup kettle. Add cold water and let stand 1 hour to draw out juices. Add carrot, turnip, celery and onion and bring slowly to simmering. Cover and cook 4 to 5 hours, adding cheesecloth spice bag last half hour. Strain broth through three thicknesses of cheesecloth, then chill to congeal fat. Bones, vegetables and spicebag may be discarded. Lift off hardened fat and re-heat broth. Season to taste with salt. Makes 1 quart Broth.

CHICKEN BROTH

1 4-to-5 pound stewing chicken	2 ribs celery, chopped
6 cups cold water	Sliced peel of 1/2 lemon
1 onion, sliced	1 bay leaf
1 carrot, sliced	Salt and pepper

Cut up chicken and cover with the cold water in the soup pot. Let stand 1 hour to draw out the juices. Add onion, carrot, celery and lemon peel. Cover and simmer 2 hours. Add bay leaf and cook 15 minutes longer. Remove chicken and chill broth to congeal fat. Lift off fat and re-heat broth. Strain. Salt and pepper to taste. Chicken meat may be used for salads or casseroles. Makes 1 quart Broth.

OXTAIL BROTH

1 oxtail	1 tablespoon Tabasco sauce
2 tablespoons flour	6 whole cloves
2 tablespoons cooking oil	6 allspice berries
2 quarts cold water	1 lemon
2 onions, chopped	1 tablespoon parsley, chopped
1 clove garlic, minced	

Cut oxtail into sections. Dredge in flour. Brown in hot oil, stirring constantly. Add onions and cook 5 minutes, stirring constantly. Put into soup kettle and add water and garlic. Cover and simmer 3 to 4 hours, adding Tabasco sauce, cloves and allspice the last half hour. Strain broth through three thicknesses of cheesecloth and chill to congeal fat. Lift off hardened fat and re-heat before serving. Season to taste with salt and pepper. Garnish with thin slices of lemon and chopped parsley. Meat may be used in meat dishes. Discard vegetables and spices. Makes 1 quart Broth.

OX CHEEK BROTH

1/2 pound lean ham, sliced
  2 tablespoons butter or
     margarine
  1 ox cheek
  6 ribs celery, chopped
  3 quarts water

  3 blades (or 1-1/2 tsp.
     ground) mace
  4 cloves
  1 bay leaf
     Salt and pepper

Brown ham lightly in butter or margarine in large soup kettle. Add ox cheek, celery and 3 quarts water. Cover and simmer 4 hours, or until meat is falling off cheek. Tie mace, cloves and bay leaf in a cheesecloth bag and add to soup kettle. Cook 15 minutes longer. Strain broth into clean container and season to taste with salt and pepper. Chill to congeal fat. Lift off hardened fat and re-heat before serving. Makes 1½ quarts Broth.

CLAM BROTH

  2 dozen fresh clams in the
     shell
  3 cups cold water

3/4 teaspoon salt
     Salted whipped cream

Clean clam shells thoroughly, using a scrub brush. Place unopened clams in a large kettle with the water and salt. Cover and bring to a boil and simmer 5 minutes, or until all shells are opened. As each is opened, place the clams in a separate dish and pour the liquor from each into the water in kettle. Strain the broth in kettle through cheesecloth and serve topped with salted whipped cream. Clams may be served with butter sauce or in a baked dish. Makes 2 cups Broth.

Consommés

Consommés are the aristocrats of the clear soups. Distilled from combinations of meats and vegetables, they are concentrated, highly-seasoned broths. Serve them elegantly in your best China soup plates as the first course for a perfect dinner.

BEEF CONSOMMÉ

2 leeks	2-1/2 quarts cold water
4 tablespoons butter or margarine	1-1/2 cups watercress, chopped
1 pound lean beef, cubed	1 small marrow bone
1 pound veal, cubed	1 bay leaf
1 3-pound chicken, cut up	1/4 teaspoon rosemary
	Salt and pepper

Chop white part of leeks and sauté in butter or margarine. Remove the leeks, set aside and brown the beef, veal and chicken lightly in the same butter. Put the browned meat and leeks in the soup kettle and add the water, watercress and marrow bone. Bring slowly to simmering. Skim off foam, cover and simmer 3 hours. Add bay leaf and rosemary and cook 15 minutes longer. Strain broth into clean kettle and chill to congeal fat. Lift off hardend fat and heat consommé. Season with salt and pepper. Meat may be used for other dishes. Makes 1¹/₂ quarts Consommé.

CURRY CONSOMMÉ

1 small onion, sliced	1 bay leaf
1 tablespoon butter or margarine	1 quart Chicken Broth
1 large sour apple	Salt and pepper
Sprig of thyme	2 tablespoons cooked rice
1 teaspoon curry powder	1 tablespoon lemon juice
Sprig of parsley	

Sauté the onion slices in butter or margarine without browning, until onion is transparent. Core and slice apple, but do not peel. Put onion, apple, thyme, curry, parsley and bay leaf into soup kettle. Stir well, then add Chicken Broth. Cover and simmer 15 minutes. Strain through three thicknesses of cheesecloth and season to taste with salt and pepper. Add rice and lemon juice and serve. Makes 1 quart Consommé.

ITALIAN CONSOMMÉ

2 tablespoons broken macaroni	2 tablespoons butter or margarine
2 cups boiling, salted water	2 cups well-seasoned Beef Consommé
4 tablespoons fresh or canned mushrooms, sliced	

Cook macaroni in boiling salted water. When tender, drain and cut into rings. Sauté mushroom slices and macaroni rings in melted butter or margarine. Add consommé, heat and serve. Makes 2 cups Consommé.

Other Clear Soups

FRENCH ONION SOUP

2 medium onions, thinly
   sliced
2 tablespoons butter or
   margarine
1 quart Beef Bouillon
   heated to boiling

Salt and pepper
4 thick slices French bread
1/4 cup grated Parmesan cheese

Sauté onion slices in butter or margarine until transparent and golden brown. Add hot Bouillon and season to taste with salt and pepper. To serve, place a slice of bread in each soup plate. Sprinkle with cheese and pour soup over it. Makes 1 quart Soup.

KIDNEY SOUP

1 beef kidney
2 tablespoons flour
2 tablespoons cooking oil
1 medium onion, sliced
4 cups Beef broth
4 cups water
1 carrot, chopped
1/2 turnip, diced

1/2 teaspoon peppercorns
   Sprig of thyme
1/2 teaspoon dried marjoram
1 bay leaf
1 blade (or 1/2 tsp. ground)
   mace
   Salt

Remove skin, wash and dry kidney. Cut meat in small pieces, discarding the core. Dust meat lightly with flour, then brown in hot cooking oil. Remove meat and set aside. Brown onion rings in oil. Place meat and onions in soup kettle and add Broth and water. Bring to a boil and skim foam off top. Add carrot, turnip and peppercorns. Simmer 4 to 5 hours. Tie thyme, marjoram, bay leaf and mace in a cheesecloth bag. Add to soup kettle and cook 30 minutes more. Season to taste with salt and pepper. Strain through three thicknesses of cheesecloth and chill broth to congeal fat. Lift off hardened fat and re-heat before serving. Discard cheesecloth bag and cooked vegetables. Kidney pieces may be saved for use in meat dishes. Makes 1 quart Soup.

RABBIT SOUP

1 rabbit	3 tablespoons butter or
2 quarts cold water	margarine
1 small onion, chopped	3 tablespoons flour
1 rib celery, sliced	1 egg yolk
1 blade (or 1/2 tsp. ground)	2 cups milk
mace	1 cup light cream
12 peppercorns	Salt
	Egg Balls

Wash and dry the rabbit and cut into pieces. Place in soup kettle and add water, onion, celery, mace and peppercorns. Cover and simmer 3 to 4 hours. Remove rabbit pieces and strain into a clean pan through three thicknesses of cheesecloth. Chill to congeal fat, then lift off hardened fat. Re-heat. In a small saucepan, lightly brown flour in melted butter or margarine. Add to soup and cook until slightly thickened. Beat the egg yolk well and add it to the milk and cream, which have been combined. Strain into the soup and stir over low heat 5 minutes more. Season to taste with salt. Add Egg Balls and serve. Rabbit meat may be used in another dish. Makes 2 quarts Soup.

GIBLET SOUP

3 sets giblets (duck, turkey or chicken)	1 small onion, chopped
1 quart cold water	2 ribs celery, sliced
1/4 pound ham, cut in small pieces	Sprig of thyme
1 carrot, chopped	Sprig of parsley
1 turnip, chopped	Sprig of marjoram
	1/2 teaspoon peppercorns

Wash giblets and chop. Add to soup kettle with water. Let stand 1 hour. Bring slowly to the simmering point and skim well. Add ham, carrot, turnip, onion and celery. Cover and simmer 3 to 4 hours. Tie thyme, parsley, marjoram and peppercorns in a piece of cheesecloth and add last half hour. Strain through three thicknesses of cheesecloth and chill until fat is congealed. Lift off hardened fat and re-heat. Season to taste with salt and pepper. Makes 1 quart Soup.

MOCK TURTLE SOUP

1 calf's liver, cut up	1 medium onion, chopped
1 calf's heart, cut up	6 peppercorns
1 small veal knuckle	3 whole cloves
2 quarts cold water	Salt

Place the liver, heart and veal knuckle in the soup kettle. Add cold water and let stand 1 hour to extract juices. Heat slowly to simmering. Add onion, peppercorns and cloves and cover. Simmer 4 to 5 hours. Strain broth into another pan and chill until fat is congealed. Lift off hardened fat and re-heat. Season to taste with salt. Makes 1 quart Soup. Liver and heart may be used in other dishes.

MADRILENE

1-1/2 cups Chicken Broth	2 ribs celery, chopped
1-1/2 cups Beef Broth	1 large carrot, chopped
1-1/2 cups tomato juice	2 leeks, white part chopped
	Salt and pepper

Combine meat broths and tomato juice. Add vegetables and simmer 30 minutes. Season to taste. Strain and re-heat. May be served hot or chilled. Makes $1^1/_2$ quarts Madrilene.

Main Dish Soups— Hot 'n Hearty

Satisfy the hearty appetites on winter days with one of these filling main-dish soups. They're not for the calorie counters in the family, but children love them. Anyway, who counts calories after a few hours of sledding or skiing?

Serve these soups for cold-weather lunches. For balanced nutrition, add a green salad or a raw vegetable relish tray and big glasses of milk.

BARLEY SOUP

2 pounds beef bones with meat scraps	4 small onions, chopped
4 quarts cold water	6 potatoes, chopped
1/2 cup uncooked barley	Sprig parsley
	Salt and pepper

Cover beef bones with cold water. Let stand 1 hour to draw out juices. Simmer 2 to 3 hours. Remove bones and set aside to cool. Strain broth into a shallow pan and chill to congeal fat. Lift off hardened fat and re-heat broth. Meanwhile, cut meat from bone in bite-size pieces, discarding bone and fat. Add meat to heated broth. Add barley and onions and cook 30 minutes. Add potatoes and cook 30 minutes more. Season to taste with salt and pepper. Garnish each bowl with chopped parsley. Makes 2^1/$_2$ quarts Soup.

BEEF-NOODLE SOUP

1 pound lean beef	1 egg yolk
1 beef bone	1/2 teaspoon salt
2 quarts cold water	1 cup flour (about)
1 medium onion, whole	2 quarts Beef Broth
8 peppercorns	Salt and pepper
1 bay leaf	Sprig parsley

Place beef and bone in soup kettle and cover with cold water. Let stand 1 hour to draw out juices. Cover and simmer 2 to 3 hours. Tie onion, peppercorns and bay leaf in a piece of cheesecloth and add to soup kettle. Cook 30 minutes longer. Meanwhile, beat egg yolk with 1/2 teaspoon salt. Working with a fork, then with the hands, add enough flour to make a very stiff dough. Roll out as thin as possible on a floured board. Let stand 10 minutes. Sprinkle lightly with flour from board and roll up, then cut the roll into thin noodle slices. Spread noodles out on countertop to dry slightly. Meanwhile, remove beef from broth and discard cheesecloth bag. Chill broth to congeal fat, then lift off hardened fat and re-heat broth to boiling. (This step may be eliminated if beef is very lean and there is no fat on bone.) Drop noodles into boiling broth gradually, so that boiling does not stop. Cover, lower heat, and cook 30 minutes, stirring occasionally to keep from sticking. Add beef, which has been cut into bite-size pieces, and 2 quarts Beef Broth (page 25). Season to taste with salt and pepper. Garnish each bowl with chopped parsley. Makes 3 quarts Soup.

BEEF-DUMPLING SOUP

1 soup bone	Salt and pepper
2 pounds stewing beef,	1-1/2 cups flour
cut up	1/2 teaspoon salt
4 quarts cold water	

Place bone and cut-up beef in soup kettle. Cover with cold water and let stand 1 hour. Heat slowly to simmering and cook 2 to 3 hours. Remove beef and bone and set aside. Season broth to taste with salt and pepper and chill to congeal fat. Lift off hardened fat. Reserve 1 cup broth and add remaining broth to soup kettle. Re-heat to boiling. Meanwhile, combine flour and $1/2$ teaspoon salt. Gradually add enough of the chilled broth to make a workable dough. Roll out as thin as possible on a floured board and cut into 3-inch squares. Drop squares, one at a time, into the boiling broth. When all squares are in the broth, lower heat, cover and cook over low heat 30 minutes, stirring occasionally to keep from sticking, but being careful not to break up the squares. Return beef pieces to soup kettle 10 minutes before serving. Makes 2 quarts Soup. Note: This soup should not be frozen or canned.

CHICKEN-RICE SOUP

1 stewing chicken, cut up	Sprig parsley
2 quarts cold water	1/2 cup uncooked rice
1 rib celery, chopped	Salt and pepper
1 onion, chopped	

Place chicken pieces in soup kettle and add cold water. Let stand 1 hour to draw out juices. Add celery, onion and parsley.

Cover and simmer 3 to 4 hours. Remove chicken from broth and set aside to cool. Strain broth and chill to congeal fat, then lift off hardened fat and re-heat broth, adding extra water to make 2 quarts. Season to taste with salt and pepper. Cut meat from chicken breast and add to broth. Remaining meat may be used in salads or casseroles or may be used to make another soup. Add rice to meat and broth. Cover and cook 30 minutes, until rice is tender. Makes 2 quarts Soup.

CHICKEN-CORN SOUP

1 stewing chicken, cut up	3 cups fresh or frozen corn
4 quarts cold water	1 cup flour
1 rib celery, chopped	1 egg
1 onion, chopped	1/4 cup water
Salt and pepper	2 hard-cooked eggs, chopped

Cover chicken with cold water and let stand 1 hour to draw out juices. Slowly bring to the simmering point. Add celery and onion and cook over low heat 3 to 4 hours. Remove chicken and strain broth into a shallow pan. Chill until fat solidifies, then lift off hardened fat and return broth to soup kettle. Reheat, and season to taste with salt and pepper. Allow chicken to cool, then cut meat into bite-size pieces. Discard bones and skin and set meat aside. Add corn to broth and simmer 5 minutes. Meanwhile, in a small bowl, combine flour, egg and 1/4 cup water. Stir with a fork, then rub togther with fingers until mixture is the size of rice kernels. Drop a few at a time into boiling soup and cook 5 minutes more. Just before serving, add chicken pieces and chopped hard-cooked eggs. Makes 2 1/2 quarts Soup.

HAM SOUP

1 ham bone	1 medium onion, whole
2 quarts cold water	Salt and pepper
3 cups raw potatoes, chopped	1 cup sour cream

Cook the ham bone in water until meat falls from the bone. Remove bone, cut meat into small pieces and return meat to broth. Add potatoes and whole onion and cook until potatoes are tender. Remove onion and discard. Season to taste with salt and pepper. Just before serving, stir in sour cream. Makes 1 1/2 quarts Soup.

CHICKEN-NOODLE SOUP

1 stewing chicken, cut up	Sprig parsley, chopped
2-1/2 quarts cold water	1 egg yolk
8 to 10 peppercorns	1/2 teaspoon salt
1/4 teaspoon anise	1 cup flour (about)
1 small whole onion	1 quart Chicken Broth
1 bay leaf	Salt and pepper
1-1/2-inch stick cinnamon	

Add chicken to soup kettle and cover with cold water. Let stand 1 hour to draw out juices. Put kettle over low heat and simmer 2 to 3 hours, adding water if necessary. Tie peppercorns, anise, whole onion, bay leaf, cinnamon stick and chopped parsley in a piece of cheesecloth and add to soup kettle. Simmer 45 minutes longer. Remove cheesecloth bag and discard. Remove chicken and set aside to cool. Chill broth to congeal fat, then lift off hardened fat and re-heat broth to boiling. Meanwhile, beat egg yolk with 1/2 teaspoon salt. Gradually add flour to make a stiff dough, then roll out as thin as possible on a floured board. Let stand 10 minutes. Sprinkle with flour from the board and roll up like a jelly roll. Cut into thin slices and spread these noodles out to dry slightly. When broth is re-heated, drop noodles into boiling broth gradually, so boiling does not stop. Lower heat, cover and simmer 45 minutes, stirring occasionally to keep from sticking. Cut chicken meat from bones and add, discarding bones and skin. Add 1 quart Chicken Broth and heat before serving. Makes 2¹/₂ quarts Soup.

GARBANZO-NOODLE SOUP

1 pound dried garbanzo beans
2 quarts cold water
  Sprig rosemary
2 quarts Brown Stock
1 egg
1/2 teaspoon salt
1 cup flour (about)

3 tablespoons butter or
  margarine
2 cloves garlic, chopped
1 small onion, chopped
1 cup tomato juice
1 hot chili pepper (fresh or
  canned) finely chopped
  Salt and pepper

Soak beans overnight in the soup kettle in water. Next day, add Brown Stock and cook beans until tender in the water in which they were soaked, adding rosemary last half hour. While beans are cooking, make noodles as follows:

Beat egg yolk with ¹/₂ teaspoon salt. Gradually add enough flour to make a very stiff dough. Roll out as thin as possible on a floured board. Let stand 10 minutes, then sprinkle with flour and roll up like a jelly roll. Cut into very thin slices. Spread out on floured surface to dry while beans cook. When they are tender, remove sprig of rosemary. In another saucepan, melt butter or margarine and sauté garlic and onion until onion is transparent but not browned. Add to the soup kettle. Add tomato juice and finely chopped hot chili. Season to taste with salt and pepper and bring to a boil. Drop noodles, a few at a time, into the boiling liquid. When all are added, lower heat and simmer over low heat 30 minutes. Makes 3 quarts Soup.

RICE-ASPARAGUS SOUP

1 small bunch fresh asparagus
1 quart Chicken Broth
1 cup water

1/2 cup uncooked rice
  Salt and pepper
  Grated cheese

Cut the tender ends of asparagus into 1-inch pieces. (Save the tougher ends for making soup stock.) Combine Chicken Broth and water and bring to a boil. Add the asparagus tops and rice. Cover and cook about 20 minutes, until rice is tender. Season to taste with salt and pepper. Garnish each bowl with grated cheese. Makes 1¹/₂ quarts Soup.

TOMATO-NOODLE SOUP

1 egg yolk	3 cups water
1/2 teaspoon salt	3 cups tomato juice
1 cup flour (about)	Salt and pepper
1 tablespoon butter or margarine	Celery salt
1 small onion, chopped	1/2 cup sour cream

Prepare the noodles by beating the egg yolk with the salt, then blending in enough flour to make a very stiff dough. Roll out thin on a floured board and let stand 10 minutes. Sprinkle with flour and roll up like a jelly roll, then cut into thin slices. Spread noodles out with the hands to partially dry while you prepare soup:

Melt butter or margarine in soup kettle and sauté onion until golden brown. Add water and tomato juice and simmer 30 minutes. Season to taste with salt, pepper and celery salt. Drop noodles into boiling liquid a few at a time so boiling does not stop, then lower heat and cover. Cook over low heat about 30 minutes. Garnish each bowl with sour cream. Makes 1¹/₂ quarts Soup.

TURKEY-MUSHROOM SOUP

2 turkey wings (or bones from leftover roast turkey)
2 quarts cold water
1 carrot, chopped
1 rib celery, chopped
1 small onion, chopped
1/4 cup uncooked rice
2 tablespoons butter or margarine
2 tablespoons flour
1 cup milk
1/4 pound fresh mushrooms (or 1 small can with juice)
1 cup cream or evaporated milk
Salt and pepper

Place turkey wings, cold water, carrot, celery and onion in soup kettle. Let stand 1 hour to draw out juices. Cover and simmer 3 to 4 hours. Strain broth into a clean kettle. Pick meat from bones and return meat to broth. Discard bones, skin and cooked vegetables. Bring broth to a boil and add uncooked rice. Cover and cook 20 minutes, until rice is tender. Meanwhile, in a saucepan, melt butter or margarine and blend in flour. Gradually add 1 cup milk and cook until thickened. Add to soup kettle. Add mushrooms which have been cleaned and cut into pieces (or canned mushrooms, juice and all). Cook 5 minutes more. Add cream or milk and season to taste with salt and pepper. Makes 1^1/$_2$ quarts Soup.

Meal-in-One-Bowl Soups

There are days when there is no time to prepare the usual meat-potatoes-vegetable meal, days when there is laundry or sewing to do, a special project to complete or a late afternoon meeting to attend.

These are the times when a meal-in-one-bowl soup can come to the rescue. It can simmer on the back of the stove while you tend to your tasks or it can be prepared a day (or days) ahead, then reheated just before dinner time. Some soup enthusiasts insist that it is better when the flavors are given a day or two to intermingle in the refrigerator between the cooking and the serving.

All of these soups contain the meat and vegetables needed for good nutrition. For a hearty meal, serve them with big chunks of fresh bread, glasses of milk, and fruit for dessert.

CHICKEN-OKRA SOUP

2 pounds chicken breasts	1 pound fresh or canned okra, sliced crosswise
4 quarts cold water	1/2 cup uncooked rice
1 medium onion, chopped	1 cup boiling water
1 green pepper, chopped	1/2 teaspoon salt
1/4 pound ham, cubed	1 teaspoon butter
8 small tomatoes, quartered	Salt and pepper

43

Cover the chicken breasts with the cold water and let stand 1 hour to draw out juices. Slowly simmer over low heat 2 hours. Remove meat from the broth and set aside to cool. Chill broth until fat congeals on top. Lift off hardened fat and reserve. Measure broth. Add water to make 3 quarts. Set aside.

When chicken breasts have cooled, cut meat into 1/2-inch cubes and discard bones and skin. Measure 6 tablespoons of the chicken fat into another saucepan and add the chopped onion and green pepper. Sauté until onions are transparent. Add cubed ham and cook until lightly browned. Heat the chicken broth in the soup kettle and add the ham-onion mixture, the chicken meat, tomatoes and okra. Cook until okra is just done. Season to taste with salt and pepper.

Meanwhile, cook rice in 1 cup boiling water and 1/2 teaspoon salt adding 1 teaspoon butter or margarine to keep it from boiling over. Tightly cover and cook over low heat 20 minutes. Place the cooked rice in a soup tureen and pour the soup over it. Serve from tureen, or place 1/4 cup cooked rice in each soup bowl and pour each serving of soup over the rice. Makes 3 quarts Soup.

CHICKEN-VEGETABLE SOUP

1 young fryer chicken, cut up	1 cup celery, chopped
3 tablespoons butter or cooking oil	1/2 cup cooked or canned tomatoes, chopped
2 quarts cold water	1 cup light cream or half-and-half
1 cup cooked green lima beans	Salt and pepper
1 cup fresh or frozen corn	

Brown chicken parts slowly in butter or oil. Place in the soup kettle and add water. Simmer 2 hours. Remove chicken and set aside to cool. Chill broth until fat congeals on top, then lift off hardened fat. Return broth to soup kettle and add lima beans, corn, celery and tomatoes. Simmer until vegetables are cooked, about 15 minutes. Meanwhile, remove chicken meat from bones and discard skin and bones. Cut meat into bite-size pieces. Add meat and cream to soup. Season to taste with salt and pepper. Makes 1^1/$_2$ quarts Soup.

HESSIAN SOUP

3 quarts cold water	6 small whole onions
1-1/2 pounds oxtails	3 ribs celery, sliced
2 cups dried split peas	1/2 teaspoon whole allspice
2 quarts cold water	4 whole cloves
3 carrots, sliced	Salt and pepper
6 turnips, sliced	3 sprigs parsley
6 potatoes, cut in bite-size pieces	

In the evening, after dinner, pour the cold water over oxtails and let stand 1 hour to draw out juices. Slowly bring to a boil and simmer 4 hours. Meanwhile, set peas to soak in the 2 quarts cold water in another pan. Before bedtime, remove the oxtails from the broth and refrigerate both separately. In the morning, lift congealed fat from meat broth and re-heat broth. Drain soaked peas and add to broth. Cook 2 hours, or until peas are soft enough to mash. Meanwhile, remove meat from oxtails, cut into bite-size pieces and discard bones and fat. Force peas through a colander or food mill and add vegetables. Tie allspice and cloves in a piece of cheesecloth and add. Cook until vegetables are tender. Discard cheesecloth bag and season soup to taste with salt and pepper. Garnish each bowl with chopped parsley. Makes 2 quarts Soup.

ENGLISH BEEF SOUP

1/2 pound tender beef, cut in
    1-inch cubes
1 small onion, cut in rings
2 tablespoons cooking oil
4 ribs celery, sliced
2 quarts Beef Broth
1/2 cup carrot, chopped

1/2 cup cooked barley
4 tablespoons flour
1 cup cold water
2 tablespoons tomato catsup
1/2 teaspoon Worcestershire
    sauce
Salt and pepper

Brown beef and onion rings in cooking oil. Add celery and Beef Broth and simmer until meat is tender. Add carrots and barley and cook 20 minutes longer. Blend flour and 1 cup cold water. Add slowly to soup kettle and simmer 5 minutes more. Add catsup, Worcestershire sauce and salt and pepper to taste. Makes 2 quarts Soup.

FAMILY SOUP

Bones and meat left over
    from beef roast
2 quarts cold water
1 medium onion, chopped
2 ribs celery, chopped
1/2 cup barley

2 medium turnips, chopped
4 medium carrots, chopped
1 1/2 cups celery, sliced
2 cups tomato juice
Salt and pepper

Put first 4 ingredients in soup kettle. Cover and simmer 2 hours. Strain broth into shallow container and set meat aside to cool. Chill broth to congeal fat. Lift off hardened fat and discard. Return broth to soup kettle. Cut meat into bite-size pieces and add to broth. Add barley to broth and simmer 1 hour. Add remaining ingredients except salt and pepper. Simmer until vegetables are tender, about 20 minutes. Season to taste with salt and pepper. Makes 2 quarts Soup.

FRENCH POT-AU-FEU

4 pounds lean rump or chuck roast	3 ribs celery
1 pound veal knuckles (or oxtail rounds)	1/2 pound leeks (white parts)
	1 medium whole onion
1 pound chicken parts (necks and backs)	2 whole cloves
	1 bay leaf
4 quarts cold water	1/4 teaspoon dried thyme
4 large carrots	8 to 10 whole peppercorns
2 medium turnips	1 medium cabbage, cut in 6 wedges
2 parsnips	Salt

In a large soup kettle, cover the beef, veal knuckles and chicken parts with water. Let stand 1 hour to draw out juices. Slowly bring to a boil and skim the foam off the top. Cover, turn the heat low and let simmer 3 to 4 hours. Strain the broth into a clean pan and chill until fat is congealed. Lift fat off and return kettle of broth to the heat. Season to taste with salt. Quarter the carrots, turnips and parsnips and cut the celery and leeks into 2-inch pieces. Add to the broth. Add the whole onion which has the 2 cloves firmly imbedded in it. Tie the bay leaf, thyme and peppercorns in a small piece of cheesecloth and immerse it in the broth. Simmer slowly until the vegetables are almost tender, about 30 minutes. Add cabbage wedges and simmer 10 minutes longer. Meanwhile, add marrow from veal knuckles or oxtail pieces and any bits of meat from the veal or chicken parts. Remove any fat from the rump or chuck roast and set it in the broth to heat in one piece. To serve, place the whole piece of beef on a platter and surround it with the vegetables. Remove and discard the whole onion and the cheesecloth spice bag. Strain the broth through three thicknesses of cheesecloth and serve in soup plates topped with croutons (page 165). Pass the meat-vegetable platter. Makes about 2 quarts Soup, plus the meat and vegetables. Note: Do not can this Soup.

HOTCH POTCH

A new version of an old Pennslyvania Dutch recipe which Grandmother called Hodge Podge or Scotch Stew:

4 quarts cold water	2 medium onions, chopped
1 pound lean beef	2 ribs celery, sliced
1 pound neck of lamb	2 turnips, chopped
Salt and pepper	1/2 cup fresh or frozen peas
1 cup green beans, cut in small pieces	1 small head cauliflower, cut in small pieces
2 carrots, chopped	1/2 head of lettuce, shredded

Add the cold water to the meats and let stand 1 hour to draw out juices. Place over low heat and simmer, covered, 2 to 3 hours. Remove meats from broth and set aside to cool. Chill broth until fat is congealed, then lift off hardened fat. Return broth to the heat and season to taste with salt and pepper. Add green beans, carrots, onions, celery and turnips. Cook until vegetables are tender. Add peas, cauliflower and lettuce and cook 20 minutes more. Add extra Beef Broth (page 25) if necessary. Makes 3 quarts Soup.

ITALIAN VEGETABLE SOUP

2 leeks	1 cup green beans, cut up
2 tablespoons olive oil or cooking oil	1 large potato, chopped
1 large onion, chopped	1 cup Italian tomatoes, chopped
1-1/2 quarts Brown Stock	1/2 cup vermicelli, broken
	Salt and pepper

Thinly slice white part of leeks. Over low heat, sauté them and chopped onion in olive oil until they are transparent, but not browned. Add Brown Stock, green beans, potato and tomatoes. Cover and simmer 30 minutes. Add vermicelli and cook 15 minutes longer. Season to taste with salt and pepper. Makes 1¹/₂ quarts Soup.

OXTAIL SOUP

2 oxtails	2 ribs celery, chopped
1/4 cup cooking oil	1 small onion, sliced
1/4 cup flour	Sprig parsley
4 quarts Brown Stock	1 bay leaf
1 cup carrot, chopped	1/2 small hot red pepper
1 cup turnip, chopped	Salt and pepper

Cut the oxtails into pieces at the joints. Sauté in the oil to a brown color. Push oxtails to one side and add flour. Blend well in oil and add 1 cup Brown Stock. Stir to blend, then add 1 quart more Stock. Pour Stock and oxtails into a large soup kettle. Add remaining Stock, cover and simmer 2 hours. Remove oxtails to a dish and set aside to cool. Chill broth until fat congeals, then lift off hardened fat and re-heat broth. Return oxtail sections to soup and add carrots, turnips, celery and onion which has been separated into rings. Tie the parsley, bay leaf and red pepper in a piece of cheesecloth and add. Simmer another 45 minutes. Remove cheesecloth bag and discard. Season to taste with salt and pepper. Makes 2 quarts Soup.

PHILADELPHIA PEPPER POT

1 knuckle of veal	1-1/2 pounds fresh white
2 large onions, sliced	honeycomb tripe
3 quarts cold water	1 teaspoon baking soda
6 whole allspice	1 teaspoon salt
10 peppercorns	2 large potatoes, chopped
2 bay leaves	2/3 cup flour
1 tablespoon sweet	1 egg
marjoram	1/2 teaspoon salt
1 tablespoon thyme	2 tablespoons butter or
1 tablespoon sweet basil	margarine
1 hot red pepper	3 tablespoons flour
	Salt and pepper

In a soup kettle place the knuckle of veal and the sliced onion. Cover with cold water and let stand 1 hour to draw juices. Bring slowly to the simmering point over low heat. Simmer 2 to 3 hours. Tie the herbs and spices in a piece of cheesecloth and add last 30 minutes. At the same time, seed and core the red pepper and cut it in tiny pieces. Add to kettle. At the end of cooking time, remove spice bag and discard. Remove knuckle from broth and set aside to cool. Keep broth hot. Clean the tripe in several waters, adding 1 teaspoon baking soda to the first water and 1 teaspoon salt to the last water. Cut with scissors into thin strips and drop into the simmering broth. Simmer 1 hour. Add potatoes and cook until tender. Meanwhile, combine the 2/3 cup flour, egg and 1/2 teaspoon salt. Roll into tiny balls with the hands and drop into the simmering broth. Let cook 30 minutes, then thicken with the butter or margarine which has been melted and mixed with the 3 tablespoons flour. Remove any meat from knuckle and chop. Add to soup, discarding bones and fat. Season to taste with salt and pepper. Makes 1¹/₂ quarts Soup.

SCOTCH BROTH

3 pounds lamb or mutton	1/4 cup celery, chopped
1/2 cup barley	1/4 cup carrots, chopped
1 teaspoon salt	1/4 cup turnips, chopped
2 quarts cold water	Salt and pepper
1/4 cup onion, chopped	

Cut meat into bite-size pieces. Put in soup kettle with barley.
Add salt and cold water. Let stand 1 hour to draw out juices,
then bring slowly to the simmering point. Cook 2 to 3 hours.
Add vegetables and simmer 30 minutes more. Season to taste
with salt and pepper. Makes 1¹/₂ quarts Soup.

RUSSIAN CABBAGE SOUP

1-1/2 pounds lean beef (chuck or rump roast) cut in small cubes

2 cups tomatoes, canned or cooked, chopped

1 large onion, chopped

1 bay leaf

1 clove garlic, minced

3 quarts cold water

1 medium head cabbage, shredded

2 tablespoons sugar

2 tablespoons vinegar

Salt and pepper

1 tablespoon lemon juice

Sour cream

Place beef, tomatoes, onion, bay leaf and garlic in soup kettle. Pour water over all and let stand 1 hour to draw out juices. Place over medium heat and simmer 2 to 3 hours. Remove bay leaf. Add cabbage, sugar and vinegar. Season to taste with salt and pepper. Simmer gently 30 minutes, or until flavors are blended. Just before serving, stir in lemon juice. Top each bowl with a heaping tablespoon of sour cream. Makes 2 quarts Soup. Note: Do not can this Soup.

SHEEP'S HEAD BROTH

1 sheep's head (or 2-1/2 pounds mutton)

2 quarts cold water

3 tablespoons barley

Salt and pepper

3 whole carrots

3 whole turnips

2 whole leeks (or onions)

1 head lettuce, quartered

Sheeps head should be well singed and split, then soaked overnight. Place in the soup kettle and cover with cold water. Add barley. Cover and simmer 4 to 5 hours, then remove head and set aside to cool. Strain broth and chill to congeal fat. Lift off hardened fat and re-heat broth. Pick meat off head and discard rest. Return meat to broth. Season to taste with salt and pepper.

Add to the kettle the whole carrots, turnips and leeks. Simmer another 45 minutes. Lay the lettuce quarters on top of the other vegetables and simmer 15 minutes more. Lift out vegetables onto serving dish with any large pieces of meat. Serve broth in soup bowls and pass the vegetable plate. Makes $1^1/_2$ quarts of Broth plus the vegetable plate.

Bean Soups

When the larder was low and it was still a long time until pay-day, Grandmother knew how to satisfy hearty appetites. She would put on a soup pot of beans or peas, for she knew that cooked, dried beans and peas supplied good nutrition and delicious flavor at low cost.

They still do. When combined with small amounts of meat, eggs or cheese in the meal, dried beans supply complete protein at far less cost than even the cheapest of meat cuts. And if you don't believe bean and pea soups can be delicious, try these:

BEAN-CHEESE SOUP

1 rib celery, chopped	1 quart Chicken Broth
1 small carrot, chopped	1/2 cup grated American or
1/2 green pepper, chopped	cheddar cheese
1 cup water	1 cup cooked Great Northern
1/4 cup butter or	or navy beans
margarine	Salt and pepper
1/4 cup flour	

Cook vegetables in the water until tender. In another saucepan, melt butter and blend in flour. Gradually add Chicken

Broth and cook over low heat until thickened. Add grated cheese and blend well. Force the cooked beans and vegetables through a colander or food mill and add to cheese sauce. Season with salt and pepper. Makes 1¹/₂ quarts Soup.

BEAN-MEATBALL SOUP

2 cups Pinto beans	2 medium carrots, sliced
2 quarts Oxtail Broth	2 cups cooked (or canned)
1 medium onion, chopped	tomatoes
2 cloves garlic, minced	Meatballs (recipe below)
1 rib celery, sliced	1-1/2 cups shredded cabbage
	Salt and pepper

Soak beans overnight in water to cover. Drain. Add Broth, onion and garlic. Cover and cook over low heat 2 hours, or until beans are tender. Add celery, carrots, tomatoes and meatballs (see below). Simmer 30 minutes longer. Add cabbage and cook until just tender. Season to taste with salt and pepper. Makes 1¹/₂ quarts Soup.

Meatballs:

1 pound ground beef	1/4 cup bread crumbs
1/4 cup onion, minced	1 teaspoon salt
2 tablespoons parsley, minced	1/8 teaspoon pepper
1 egg	1/4 teaspoon oregano

Blend all ingredients well. Shape into 24 small meatballs and brown in hot cooking oil.

BEAN-PEA SOUP

1 cup dried pinto beans	with scraps of meat
1 cup dried navy beans	3 ribs celery, sliced
2 cups dried split peas	2 small onions, thinly sliced
3-1/2 quarts cold water	3 carrots, diced
8 whole peppercorns	1/4 teaspoon dry mustard
2 ham hocks or a ham bone	Salt

Soak beans and peas overnight in water to cover. Drain and cover with 3½ quarts fresh water. Tie peppercorns in a piece of cheesecloth and add. Add all remaining ingredients except salt. Simmer, covered, over low heat until beans are tender and soup is slightly thickened, 3 or 4 hours. Remove bone and cut off meat. Discard bone, skin and fat, and chop meat fine. Return meat to soup. Season to taste with salt. Makes 3 quarts Soup.

BEAN AND SPINACH SOUP

1 cup dried Navy beans	2 tablespoons butter or
2 quarts White Stock	margarine
1 bay leaf	1 tablespoon flour
1 medium onion, chopped	2 cups chopped spinach, cooked
1 clove garlic, minced	Salt and pepper

Soak beans overnight in water to cover. Drain. Add White Stock, bay leaf, onion and garlic. Cover and cook over low heat until beans are tender. Melt butter in another saucepan and blend in flour. Add a bit of the soup liquid and stir until well blended. Add to the soup stock and cook until slightly thickened. Add spinach. Season to taste with salt and pepper. Makes 1$^{1}/_{2}$ quarts Soup.

BLACK BEAN SOUP

2 cups Black beans	1-1/2 tablespoons flour
2 quarts cold water	Salt and pepper
3 tablespoons butter or	1/4 teaspoon dry mustard
margarine	Few grains cayenne
1 small onion, sliced	2 hard-cooked eggs
2 ribs celery, chopped	1 lemon

Soak beans overnight in water to cover. Drain and add 2 quarts cold water. In a skillet, heat half the butter or margarine and sauté the onions slices in this. Add to the beans and water. Add celery and cook 3 or 4 hours, until beans are soft. Add more water if necessary during cooking. Mash beans with a potato masher while in the soup. In a cup, blend flour, salt, pepper, mustard and cayenne with remaining butter, then add to beans and cook over low heat, stirring well, until thickened. Cut eggs and lemon into very thin slices and top each serving bowl with an egg slice and a lemon slice. Makes 1$^{1}/_{2}$ quarts Soup.

CREAM OF BEAN SOUP

2 cups dried white beans
  (Great Northern, lima,
  navy, etc.)
5 cups cold water
6 cups ham broth

1 tablespoon flour
1 cup cream or rich milk
1/4 cup parsley, chopped
  Salt and pepper

Let beans soak overnight in water to cover. Drain and add 5 cups cold water and ham broth. Cook over low heat until beans are very tender. Mash through a colander or food mill to remove bean shells. Add $^1/_2$ cup soup broth to 1 tablespoon flour. Blend well, then add to soup. Stir in cream and simmer, stirring, until soup is smooth and creamy. Season to taste with salt and pepper. Garnish each bowl with parsley. Makes $2^1/_2$ quarts Soup. Note: Do not freeze or can this soup.

DRIED BEAN SOUP

2 cups dried Great Northern or
  navy beans
3 quarts cold water
4 quarts boiling water
1 tablespoon celery, chopped

1 large onion, minced
4 tablespoons butter or
  margarine
3 tablespoons flour
  Salt and pepper

Soak beans overnight in cold water to cover. Drain. Add 3 quarts cold water and bring to a boil. Drain again. Add 4 quarts boiling water and simmer over low heat until beans are tender. Add celery and cook until soup is thickened. Meanwhile, in a skillet sauté the chopped onion in the butter or margarine. Add the flour and blend well, then stir in a small amount of bean broth. Stir well, add more broth and cook until thickened. Add to soup and mash half of the beans with a potato masher. Season to taste with salt and pepper. Makes $2^1/2$ quarts Soup.

KIDNEY BEAN SOUP

1 cup dried kidney beans
4 cups cold water
2 tablespoons onion, chopped
   Sprig parsley
1 rib celery, chopped
1 small carrot, chopped

4 tablespoons butter or
   margarine
2 tablespoons flour
3 cups tomato juice
1 teaspoon Worcestershire sauce
   Salt and pepper
   Dash of cayenne

Soak beans overnight in water to cover. Drain. Add 4 cups cold water, onion, parsley, celery and carrot. Cook over low heat until tender. Remove parsley sprig and mash beans with a potato masher. In a small skillet, melt butter or margarine and blend in flour. Gradually stir in tomato juice and Worcestershire sauce. Cook until thickened. Blend into soup. Season to taste with salt, pepper and cayenne. Makes 1 quart Soup.

LENTIL SOUP

1 cup lentils
8 cups water
1 ham bone
1 large onion, sliced

2 ribs celery, chopped
   Salt and pepper
2 wieners, sliced in rings

Soak lentils overnight in water to cover. Drain. Add 8 cups water, ham bone, onion and celery. Cover and cook over low heat 2 hours, until lentils are soft. Remove ham bone and season soup to taste with salt and pepper. Serve with sliced wieners as a garnish. Makes 1 quart Soup.

LIMA BEAN SOUP

1-1/2 cups dried lima beans
  2 quarts water or meat stock
  2 tablespoons butter or
     margarine

2 tablespoons flour
  Salt and pepper
  Celery salt
1 tablespoon onion juice

Soak beans overnight in water to cover. Drain. Add 2 quarts water or stock and cook over low heat until beans are soft. Force through a colander or food mill to remove bean shells and thicken with a mixture of the butter or margarine and flour. Season to taste with salt, pepper, celery salt and onion juice. Makes $1^1/_2$ quarts Soup.

NAVY BEAN SOUP

1 cup dried navy beans
5 cups cold water
1 ham bone, with meat scraps
1 carrot
1 turnip

1 large onion
2 potatoes
2 cups cold water
  Salt and pepper

Cover beans with cold water and soak overnight. Drain. Add 5 cups water and ham bone and cook, covered, until beans are tender. Remove ham bone. Discard bone and fat. Chop meat and return to soup kettle. Run carrot, turnip, onion and potatoes through blender with 2 cups cold water. (Or chop very fine, then add water.) Add to beans and cook 1 hour longer, or until beans are soft and soup is thickened. Season to taste with salt and pepper. Makes 3 quarts Soup.

OLD FASHIONED NEW ENGLAND
BEAN SOUP

2 cups pea beans	1 small onion, chopped
6 cups cold water	1 carrot, chopped
1/4 pound lean salt pork, cut up	Salt and pepper
1/2 rib celery, chopped	

Soak beans overnight in water to cover. Drain. Add 6 cups cold water, the salt pork, celery, onion and carrot. Cover and cook over low heat until the beans are tender. Season to taste with salt and pepper. Makes 1^1/$_2$ quarts Soup.

PEA-TOMATO SOUP

1 cup dried Yellow Split peas	1 teaspoon celery salt
2 cups fresh or canned tomatoes	Salt and pepper
4 cups water	Lemon slices
1 medium onion, sliced	Fresh green peas
1 rib celery, chopped	

Soak dried peas overnight in water to cover. In the morning, drain and add tomatoes, water, onion and celery. Cook until peas are tender. Force through a colander or food mill and add celery salt. Season to taste with salt and pepper. Garnish bowls with thin slices of lemon and a few fresh green peas. Makes 1 quart Soup.

QUICK SPLIT PEA SOUP

1 cup dried split peas	3 tablespoons celery, chopped
5 cups White Stock	1 carrot, diced
2 tablespoons onion, chopped	Salt and pepper

Combine all ingredients and cook over low heat until peas are tender. Season to taste with salt and pepper, and spin through the blender. Makes 1 quart Soup.

SPLIT PEA SOUP

1 cup dried split peas	3 tablespoons butter or
3 quarts cold water	margarine
1 ham bone	3 tablespoons flour
1 tablespoon onion, chopped	2 cups milk
	Salt and pepper

Soak peas overnight in water to cover. Drain. Cover with 3 quarts water. Add ham bone and onion. Cook until peas are soft. Melt butter or margarine and blend in flour. Add to it a small amount of soup and stir well, then add back to soup kettle. Add milk and cook, stirring constantly, until soup thickens. Season to taste with salt and pepper. Makes 2 quarts Soup.

TANGY BEAN SOUP

1 cup dried beans (navy, lentils or limas)	2 tablespoons flour
6 cups cold water	1/8 teaspoon dry mustard
1 small onion, chopped	4 teaspoons vinegar
1 carrot, sliced	2 teaspoons brown sugar
1 tablespoon butter or margarine	1 hard-cooked egg
	Salt and pepper

Soak beans overnight in water to cover. Drain. Add 6 cups cold water, onion and carrot. Cover and cook over low heat 2 hours, or until beans are tender. In another pan, melt butter or margarine and blend in flour. Add to beans along with mustard, vinegar and brown sugar. Cook, stirring constantly, until thickened. Season to taste with salt and pepper. Garnish with chopped hard-cooked egg. Makes 2 quarts Soup.

RED POTTAGE SOUP

1 cup haricot or other white beans	1 raw beet, whole
6 cups cold water	1 rib celery, chopped
4 tomatoes (fresh or canned)	1 medium onion, chopped
	Salt and pepper

Soak beans overnight in water to cover. Drain. Add 6 cups cold water, the tomatoes, beet (left whole), celery and onion. Cover and cook over low heat 3 or 4 hours, until beans are tender. Remove the beet and discard. Force the rest through a colander or food mill. Season to taste with salt and pepper. Makes 1$^{1}/_{2}$ quarts Soup.

TOMATO-BEAN SOUP

2 cups dried navy beans	4 sprigs parsley
5 cups cold water	1/4 teaspoon dried marjoram
Lamb (or pork) bones	1/2 cup onion, chopped
1 clove garlic, cut in half	2 cups tomatoes, canned or
8 to 10 peppercorns	cooked
1 bay leaf	Salt and pepper

Set beans to soak in enough water to cover overnight, then drain. Add 5 cups cold water and meat bones. Tie garlic, peppercorns, bay leaf, parsley, marjoram and onion in a piece of

cheesecloth and set aside. Add tomatoes to beans and simmer
gently 3 or 4 hours, adding cheesecloth bag last 30 minutes.
Remove bones and cheesecloth bag and mash beans with a
potato masher. Cut any bits of meat off bone and return to soup.
Season to taste with salt and pepper. Makes 2¹/₂ quarts Soup.

VEGETABLE-BEAN SOUP

1 small carrot, chopped
1 cup green peas
1 tomato, chopped
1 turnip, chopped
2 tablespoons uncooked rice

1 quart Beef Broth
1 cup cooked beans (any kind)
1 quart water
   Salt and pepper

Add carrots, peas, tomato, turnip and rice to Beef Broth and
cover. Cook over low heat until rice is cooked and vegetables
are tender. Add beans and water. Season to taste with salt and
pepper. Makes 2¹/₂ quarts Soup.

All-Vegetable Soups

For good nutrition at low cost, nothing is better than all-vegetable soups. They're ideal for the reluctant vegetable eaters in the family and excellent for those who are especially fond of vegetables.

Serve any of these soups for a light, yet satisfying lunch or supper, with sandwiches or as a delicious beginning to a vegetable-light meal.

BORSHT

1/2 pound raw beets	1 cup cabbage, shredded
2 large carrots	2 garlic cloves, minced
2 medium onions, chopped	1 bay leaf
3 cups water	2 tablespoons lemon juice
2 cups Beef Bouillon	Salt and pepper
or Vegetable Bouillon	Sour cream

Clean beets and carrots well. Cut off beet tops, leaving two inches of stem. Scrape carrots, but leave whole. Place both in soup kettle. Add chopped onions and water. Cover and simmer 20 minutes. Remove beets, slip off skins and return to kettle. Add Bouillon, cabbage, garlic and bay leaf. Cover and cook 15 minutes longer. Force vegetables through a colander or food mill and add lemon juice. Season to taste with salt and pepper. Top each serving with a spoonful of sour cream. Borsht also may be served chilled: see page 133. Makes 1 quart Soup.

CABBAGE SOUP

1 small cabbage, shredded	2 tablespoons flour
2 cups water	2 cups milk
3 slices onion	Salt and pepper
4 tablespoons butter or margarine	Few grains cayenne

Cook cabbage in water until tender. Force through a colander or food mill. In another pan, sauté onion in butter or margarine until transparent. Stir in flour, then add milk and cabbage mixture. Cook 5 minutes. Season to taste with salt, pepper and cayenne. Makes 1 quart Soup. Note: Do not can this Soup.

CARROT SOUP

3 tablespoons butter or margarine	2 quarts Chicken Broth
2 pounds carrots, scraped and sliced	Salt and pepper

Melt butter or margarine in soup kettle. Add carrot slices and cook over low heat 1 hour. Stir occasionally, but keep heat low enough that carrots will not brown. Add Chicken Broth and cook 15 minutes longer. Force through a colander or food mill or spin through a blender. Season to taste with salt and pepper. Makes 1¹/₂ quarts Soup.

CORN-TOMATO SOUP

2 cups cooked or canned corn
1 cup fresh or canned
  tomatoes
2 cups celery, sliced
1 quart cold water
2 tablespoons butter or
  margarine

3 tablespoons flour
1 cup milk
1/2 cup grated cheese
1/2 cup pimiento, chopped
  Salt and pepper

Combine corn, tomatoes, celery and water in soup kettle and cook 30 minutes. In a saucepan, melt butter or margarine and blend in flour. Gradually add milk and cook until thickened, stirring constantly. Add to soup kettle and stir well. Add cheese and pimiento and stir until cheese is melted. Season to taste with salt and pepper. Makes 2 quarts Soup.

CUCUMBER SOUP

1 large cucumber
1 teaspoon salt
1 tablespoon butter or
  margarine

1 quart White Stock
  Salt and pepper
2 egg yolks
1-1/2 cups light cream

Peel and quarter cucumber. Remove seeds, then cut in thin slices. Sprinkle with 1 teaspoon salt and let stand 1 hour. Drain. Melt butter or margarine in saucepan and add cucumber slices. Over very low heat, let cook 15 minutes, but do not allow to brown. Add White Stock and simmer 45 minutes. Season to taste with salt and pepper. In a mixing bowl, beat the egg yolks well and add the cream. Pour into the soup just before serving. Makes 1^1/$_2$ quarts Soup.

GREEN BEAN SOUP

2 cups canned green beans	1 teaspoon dried summer
1 small onion, chopped	savory
1-1/2 cups diced potatoes	1/2 cup light cream
2 quarts ham broth or	1 tablespoon butter or
White Stock	margarine
2 teaspoons chopped dried	Salt and pepper
parsley	

Combine green beans, onion and potatoes. Add broth or stock. Tie parsley and summer savory in a piece of cheesecloth. Cover and simmer 45 minutes. Remove cheesecloth bag. Just before serving, add cream and butter or margarine. Season to taste with salt and pepper. Makes 2^{1}/$_{2}$ quarts Soup.

HERB SOUP

4 tablespoons butter or	1 leek, blanched and sliced
margarine	4 medium potatoes, chopped
1 cup spinach, finely chopped	2 quarts boiling water
1/2 cup sorrel, shredded	1 tablespoon chervil, chopped
1 head lettuce, shredded	Salt and pepper

Melt butter or margarine in the soup kettle and add spinach, sorrel, lettuce and white part of leek. Cook 15 minutes, but do not let the vegetables brown. Add potatoes and boiling water. Cover and simmer 1 hour. At the end of that time, mash potatoes, add the chervil and simmer 5 minutes longer. Season to taste with salt and pepper. Makes 2 quarts Soup.

LEEK SOUP

2 tablespoons butter or
   margarine
2 cups leeks, chopped
4 tablespoons onion, minced

3 quarts boiling water
4 cups chopped potatoes
   Salt and pepper

Melt the butter or margarine in the soup kettle and add white part of leeks and onion. Cook over low heat 20 minutes, stirring frequently, until transparent and golden but not brown. Add the boiling water and potatoes and cook 30 minutes longer. Season to taste with salt and pepper. Makes 2 quarts Soup.

LETTUCE SOUP

1 large head lettuce, shredded
1 slice of onion
1 slice of green pepper
1 small carrot, sliced

1 quart White Stock
   or Chicken Broth
   Salt and pepper
2 tablespoons flour

Remove the outer leaves of lettuce and reserve. Shred the remainder. Simmer shredded lettuce, onion, green pepper and carrot in Stock or Broth 30 minutes in covered soup kettle. Strain into clean container, force vegetables through a colander or food mill and return pulp to soup. Season to taste with salt and pepper and add remaining lettuce, shredded very fine. Cook 30 minutes more. Meanwhile, combine 2 tablespoons flour with 1/2 cup of the soup. Return to soup kettle and stir until slightly thickened. Makes 1 1/2 quarts Soup.

SOUP NORMANDIE

1 onion, chopped	1 tablespoon cornstarch
2 tablespoons butter or margarine	1 tablespoon cold water
	1 tablespoon sugar
4 cups tomatoes, cooked or canned	12 whole cloves
	Salt and pepper
1 quart cold water	Dash of Tabasco sauce

Sauté the onion in the melted butter or margarine until transparent but not browned. Add tomatoes and water and simmer 20 minutes. Force through a colander or food mill. Blend cornstarch with 1 tablespoon cold water to make a paste. Add to soup. Stir in sugar and cloves. Let cook 5 minutes more, then strain out cloves and season to taste with salt, pepper, and Tabasco. Makes $1^{1}/_{2}$ quarts Soup.

ONION SOUP

5 medium onions, sliced	3 tablespoons flour
5 tablespoons butter or margarine	2 cups milk
	1 egg yolk
2 cups White Stock	Salt and pepper

Over low heat sauté onions in 2 tablespoons butter or margarine until transparent but not browned. Add Stock and cook 30 minutes. Force through a colander or food mill. In another pan, melt remaining 3 tablespoons butter or margarine and blend in flour. Gradually add milk, mix thoroughly and add the egg yolk. Cook until thickened. Add to onion mixture and season to taste with salt and pepper. Makes 1 quart Soup.

OKRA SOUP

3 pounds beef with bone
1/2 pound lean ham
3 quarts cold water
4 cups fresh or canned okra, sliced

3 pounds tomatoes, peeled and quartered
2 cups corn, fresh or frozen
Salt and pepper

Put the beef and ham in the soup kettle and cover with 3 quarts cold water. Let stand 1 hour to draw out juices. Cover and simmer 2 to 3 hours. Strain liquid into a shallow pan and chill to congeal fat. Lift off hardened fat and reheat stock in soup kettle. Meanwhile, separate ham and beef from fat and bones. Discard fat and bones and cut meat into bite-size pieces. Return to reheated stock. Add okra, tomatoes and corn and simmer until well cooked and the flavors have blended, about 1 hour. Season to taste with salt and pepper. Makes 2 quarts Soup.

RUTABAGA-CHEESE SOUP

2 cups grated raw rutabaga (about 1 pound)
1 cup water
2 tablespoons butter or margarine
3 tablespoons flour
1-3/4 cups milk
2 cups Chicken Broth

1/3 pound (1-1/2 cups) grated American or cheddar cheese
3/4 teaspoon seasoning salt
1/2 teaspoon sugar
1 tablespoon parsley, chopped

Cook rutabaga in water 8 minutes, until tender. Melt butter or margarine in another pan and blend in flour. Gradually add milk and cook, stirring constantly, until thickened. Add cooked rutabaga, Chicken Broth, cheese and seasonings. Stir and reheat. Garnish with choppped parsley. Makes 1 quart Soup.

SORREL SOUP

1/2 cup sorrel, shredded	2 egg yolks
3 tablespoons butter or margarine	3 tablespoons milk
1-1/2 quarts boiling water	Salt and pepper

Cook shredded sorrel in $1^1/_2$ tablespoons butter or margarine 5 minutes, stirring frequently to keep from browning. Add water and simmer 10 minutes. Meanwhile, in another pan beat the egg yolks, add the milk and remaining butter or margarine. Gradually pour the hot soup into this and heat well. Season to taste with salt and pepper. Makes $1^1/_2$ quarts Soup.

SPINACH SOUP

1 pound fresh spinach, chopped	3 tablespoons flour
1 quart Chicken Broth	2 cups milk
3 tablespoons butter or margarine	Salt and pepper

Wash spinach but do not drain. Cook over low heat, in a tightly-covered saucepan in only the water that clings to the leaves. When just done, chop fine and force through a colander or food mill. Add pulp and cooking water to Chicken Broth. In another pan, melt butter or margarine and blend in flour. Gradually add milk and cook until thickened. Add to spinach-Broth mixture. Season to taste with salt and pepper. Makes $1^1/_2$ quarts Soup.

TOMATO SOUP

3 tablespoons butter or
  margarine
2 tablespoons flour
4 cups cooked or canned
  tomatoes
2 slices onion
2 sprigs parsley

1 bay leaf
  Grating of nutmeg (or 1/8
  teaspoon powdered)
3 whole cloves
4 cups water
  Salt, pepper and cayenne

Melt butter or margarine and blend in flour. Set aside. Combine in soup kettle the tomatoes and water and the onion, parsley, bay leaf, nutmeg and cloves, tied in a piece of cheesecloth. Simmer 20 minutes. Remove cheesecloth bag. Force through a colander or food mill, then add flour mixture. Cook 5 minutes. Season to taste with salt, pepper and cayenne. Makes 1 quart Soup.

TOMATO-BARLEY SOUP

2 medium onions, chopped
4 tablespoons butter or
  margarine
4 cups canned tomatoes

2 quarts boiling water
1 cup barley
  Salt and pepper

Sauté the chopped onions in the butter or margarine until transparent but not browned. Add tomatoes, boiling water and barley and cook 1 hour over low heat. Add salt and pepper to taste. Makes 3 quarts Soup.

TOMATO-CHEESE SOUP

1 medium onion, thinly sliced
3 tablespoons butter or
    margarine
2 cups canned tomatoes
3 cups Beef Broth

1/2 teaspoon oregano
      Salt and pepper
1 cup shredded American or
    cheddar cheese

Sauté onion in butter until transparent but not browned. Add tomatoes, Beef Broth and oregano and simmer 30 minutes. Force through a colander or food mill. Season to taste with salt and pepper. Top each bowlful with grated cheese. Makes 1 quart Soup.

TOMATO-OKRA SOUP

1/4 cup uncooked rice
4 cups water
1-1/2 tablespoons butter or
    margarine
3 tablespoons onion,
    chopped
1/2 green pepper, chopped

2 ribs celery, chopped
2 cups cooked or canned
    tomatoes
2 cups okra pods, sliced
    Salt and pepper
    Sprig parsley, chopped

Pour the uncooked rice in a small, dry skillet and place over low heat. Stir constantly until the rice is a light, golden color. Pour into the soup kettle, add water and bring to a boil. In the same skillet, melt the butter or margarine and sauté the onion, green pepper and celery over low heat until onion is transparent but not browned, about 10 minutes. When rice is tender, add the sautéed vegetable mixture, tomatoes and sliced okra. Simmer until okra is cooked to desired doneness. Season to taste with salt and pepper. Garnish each bowl with chopped parsley. Makes 1¹/₂ quarts Soup.

VEGETARIAN VEGETABLE SOUP

1   medium potato
1   medium carrot
1   cup shredded kale or
    cabbage
1   medium onion
1/2 rib celery

2   quarts water
1   cup oatmeal
1   cup milk
1   tablespoon butter or
    margarine
    Salt and pepper

Chop the potato, carrot, kale or cabbage, onion and celery with the coarse blade of a food grinder. Add to the soup kettle and simmer 15 minutes over medium heat in 2 quarts water. Add the oatmeal and cook until oatmeal is done. Add milk and butter or margarine, and season to taste with salt and pepper. Makes 2^1/$_2$ quarts Soup. Note: Do not can this soup.

Cream Soups

Cream soups are especially appropriate foods for children, the elderly and invalids, or for those family members who may not drink enough milk. Included here also is a group of "Try-Something-Different" soups—Buttermilk, Cheese, Chestnut, Egg, Peanut Butter, Rivel and Vinegar soups.

Serve these cream soups alone as a light meal or with a salad or sandwiches for supper. To cut costs, use diluted evaporated milk or reconstituted powdered milk to replace all or part of the milk called for in the recipes.

Remember that Cream Soups are not suitable for canning or freezing.

CREAM OF ARTICHOKE SOUP

2 cups cut up Jerusalem artichokes	2 tablespoons flour
1 slice onion	2 cups milk
3 cups cold water	1 egg, beaten
2 tablespoons butter or margarine	Salt and pepper
	Cayenne

Cook artichokes and onion in water until tender. Drain, reserving cooking water. Force vegetables through a colander or food mill and return to water. In another pan, melt butter or margarine and stir in flour. Gradually add milk, stirring constantly. Add beaten egg and cook over low heat until sauce thickens. Add to artichoke pulp mixture and blend well. Season to taste with salt, pepper and cayenne. Makes $1^1/_2$ quarts Soup.

CREAM OF ASPARAGUS SOUP

2 pounds fresh asparagus, cut up	3 tablespoons butter or margarine
4 cups liquid (water or vegetable cooking water)	3 tablespoons flour
1/4 cup onion, chopped	1/2 cup cream or evaporated milk
1/2 cup celery, chopped	2 cups Chicken Broth
	Salt and pepper

Wash and drain asparagus. Place in kettle containing 4 cups liquid, onion and celery. Cover and simmer 20 to 30 minutes, until tender. Lift asparagus out of liquid and force as much as possible through a colander or food mill. Return purée to liquid. In another pan, melt the butter or margarine and blend in flour. Gradually add cream or evaporated milk and cook, stirring constantly, over low heat until mixture is thickened. Add Chicken Broth. Add to asparagus mixture and blend well. Cook 5 minutes, stirring constantly. Season to taste with salt and pepper. Makes 2 quarts Soup.

BUTTERMILK SOUP

1 quart cultured buttermilk	1/2 cup flour
1 egg	Salt and pepper

Heat buttermilk to scalding in the top of a double boiler. Beat egg well and blend in the flour. Gradually add 1/2 cup hot buttermilk to egg-flour mixture, then add back to buttermilk. Stir to blend well. Season to taste with salt and pepper and serve hot. Makes 1 quart Soup.

CREAM OF CARROT SOUP

4 large carrots, sliced	3 tablespoons flour
2 cups water	3-1/2 cups milk
3 tablespoons butter or	Salt and pepper
margarine	

Cook carrot slices in 2 cups water until soft enough to force through a colander or food mill. In a large saucepan, melt butter or margarine and blend in flour. Gradually add milk, stirring constantly, and cook until thickened. Add carrot pulp and season to taste with salt and pepper. Makes 1^1/2 quarts Soup.

CREAM OF CAULIFLOWER SOUP

1 medium cauliflower
4 cups cold water
2 slices onion
4 tablespoons butter or
   margarine

4 tablespoons flour
2 cups milk
2 tablespoons grated cheese
1 egg yolk
   Salt and pepper

Cook cauliflower in water until very tender. Drain, reserving liquid. Force cauliflower through a colander or food mill and return to liquid. In a small saucepan, sauté onion in butter or margarine until onion is transparent, about 10 minutes. Blend in flour. Gradually add milk and cook, stirring constantly, until thickened. Add cheese and egg yolk. Cook, stirring, until cheese is melted. Add to cauliflower mixture. Season to taste with salt and pepper. Makes $1^1/_2$ quarts Soup.

CREAM OF CELERIAC SOUP

4 cups celeriac, chopped
4 cups White Stock
   or Chicken Broth
2 tablespoons butter or

   margarine
1 tablespoon flour
1 cup cream or evaporated milk
   Salt and pepper

Cook the celeriac 30 minutes in the stock or broth. Drain, reserving liquid. Force celeriac through a colander or food mill. Return to stock. In another pan, melt butter or margarine and blend in flour. Gradually add cream or evaporated milk and cook, stirring constantly, until thickened. Add to celeriac mixture. Season to taste with salt and pepper. Makes $1^1/_2$ quarts Soup.

CREAM OF CELERY SOUP

2 cups celery, chopped
1 tablespoon green pepper, chopped
2 cups White Stock
1 tablespoon butter or margarine

1 tablespoon flour
1 cup milk
3/4 cup cream or evaporated milk
Salt and pepper

Cook celery and green pepper 30 minutes in Stock. Meanwhile, in another pan, melt the butter or margarine and blend in the flour. Gradually add enough soup liquid to make a smooth paste, then add back to the soup. Stir and simmer until smooth and thickened. When vegetables are tender, add milk and cream or evaporated milk. Season to taste with salt and pepper. Makes $1^1/_2$ quarts Soup.

CREAM OF CHEESE SOUP

1/4 cup onion, finely chopped
4 tablespoons butter or margarine
4 tablespoons flour
4 cups milk

1 cup grated process cheese
1/2 cup cooked green peas
1/4 cup red bell pepper, chopped
Salt and pepper

Sauté onion in butter or margarine over low heat until onion is transparent but not browned. Blend in the flour and gradually add 2 cups of the milk. Cook, stirring constantly, until thickened. Add remaining milk, stirring to blend. Add cheese and cook and stir until cheese melts. Add peas and sweet bell pepper and season to taste with salt and pepper. Makes 1 quart Soup.

CHESTNUT SOUP

4 cups chestnuts, shelled and
  blanched
2 cups White Stock
  or Chicken Broth

2 tablespoons butter or
  margarine
2 tablespoons flour
2 cups milk
  Salt and pepper

Cook chestnuts in Stock or Broth until soft. Strain, reserving liquid. Force chestnuts through a colander or food mill, then return pulp to Stock. In another pan, melt butter or margarine and blend in the flour. Gradually add milk and cook, stirring constantly, until thickened. Add to chestnut mixture. Season to taste with salt and pepper. Makes 1 quart Soup.

QUICK CREAM OF CHICKEN SOUP

2 tablespoons butter or
  margarine
3 tablespoons flour
3 cups Chicken Broth
1 cup light cream or diluted
  evaporated milk

1/2 cup leftover chicken,
  finely chopped
  Salt and pepper
1 teaspoon chives, chopped

Melt butter or margarine in saucepan and blend in flour. Gradually add Chicken Broth and cook, stirring constantly, until thickened. Add cream or evaporated milk and chicken and stir until well blended. Season to taste with salt and pepper and garnish with chopped chives. Makes 1 quart Soup.

CREAM OF CHICKEN SOUP

1 stewing chicken, cut up	4 tablespoons butter or
2 ribs celery	margarine
1 medium onion, chopped	4 tablespoons flour
2 sprigs parsley	2 cups light cream or evaporated
1 bay leaf	milk
8 cups cold water	Salt and pepper

Place chicken, celery, onion, parsley and bay leaf in soup kettle. Pour the cold water over all and let stand 1 hour. Cover and simmer 3 to 4 hours. Lift out chicken to cool. Strain broth. Chill broth to congeal fat, then lift off hardened fat and re-heat liquid. Finely chop enough white meat to make 2 cups meat and add to soup stock. (Remainder of the chicken may be used for other recipes.) In another pan, melt butter or margarine and blend in flour. Gradually add cream or evaporated milk and cook until thickened, stirring constantly. Re-heat, stirring to blend well. Add to soup stock. Season to taste with salt and pepper. Makes 1¹/₂ quarts Soup.

CREAM OF CORN SOUP

6 to 8 ears fresh sweet corn	2 tablespoons butter or
3 cups cold water	margarine
1 tablespoon sugar	Salt and pepper
1 cup cream or evaporated milk	

Remove husks from corn, rub off silks, cut away any bad places and, using a sharp paring knife, cut through all the kernels to slice them open. Do not cut the kernels off the cobs. Place the ears in the soup kettle, cover with the cold water. Cover kettle and simmer 6 to 8 minutes. Remove the ears, reserving the cooking water. Scrape the ears with a blunt knife to remove the pulp, but leaving the kernel shells on the ear. Return the pulp to cooking water. Discard the ears. Add sugar, cream or **evaporated** milk and butter. Season to taste with salt and pepper. Heat just to boiling. Garnish bowls with popped corn. Makes 1 quart Soup.

CREAM OF CUCUMBER SOUP

4 cucumbers, peeled and chopped	4 tablespoons butter or
4 ribs celery, chopped	margarine
2 slices onion	4 tablespoons flour
1 tablespoon green pepper,	2 cups milk
chopped	1 cup cream or evaporated milk
2 cups Chicken Broth	Salt and pepper

Cook cucumbers, celery, onion and green pepper in Broth 20 minutes, or until tender. Strain, reserving liquid. Force vegetables through a colander or food mill and return to Broth. In a saucepan melt butter or margarine and blend in flour. Gradually add 2 cups of the soup stock and the milk. Cook, stirring constantly, until thickened. Add to soup. Add cream or evaporated milk and blend well. Season to taste with salt and pepper. Makes $1^1/_2$ quarts Soup.

EGG SOUP

4 cups milk	Salt and pepper
3 eggs, well beaten	2 cups toasted bread crumbs

Scald milk and gradually add eggs, stirring constantly. Season to taste with salt and pepper. Just before serving, top each bowl with toasted bread crumbs. Makes $1^1/_2$ quarts Soup.

CREAM OF GREEN BEAN SOUP

2 cups canned green beans
3 tablespoons butter or
  margarine
2 tablespoons onion, chopped
2 tablespoons flour

2 cups milk
1/2 cup cream or evaporated
    milk
Salt and pepper

Force green beans through colander or food mill, retaining liquid in which they were canned. Return strained pulp to liquid and heat. Meanwhile, melt butter or margarine in a saucepan. Sauté onions until they are transparent but not browned. Blend in flour and gradually add milk. Cook until thickened and smooth, stirring constantly. Add to bean mixture and heat thoroughly. Add cream or evaporated milk. Season to taste with salt and pepper. Makes 1 quart Soup.

CREAM OF MUSHROOM SOUP

1/4 pound fresh mushrooms or
    1/2 cup canned mushrooms
2 tablespoons butter or
  margarine
1 tablespoon flour

1 cup Chicken Broth
2 cups milk
1/2 cup cream or evaporated
    milk
Salt and pepper

Finely chop mushrooms and sauté in butter or margarine 5 minutes over low heat. Cover and cook 5 minutes longer. Blend in flour. Gradually add Chicken Broth and cook, stirring constantly, until thickened. Add milk and simmer 2 minutes more. Reduce heat, add cream or evaporated milk and heat 2 minutes more. Season to taste with salt and pepper. Makes 1 quart Soup.

MOCK OYSTER SOUP

1-1/2 cups salsify, chopped	3 cups milk
1-1/2 cups water	1/2 cup cream or evaporated
1 tablespoon butter or	milk
margarine	Salt and pepper

Cook salsify in water until tender. Add butter or margarine, milk and cream or evaporated milk and bring just to simmering. Season to taste with salt and pepper. Makes 1 quart Soup.

CREAM OF ONION SOUP

6 medium onions, chopped	1 egg yolk, slightly beaten
8 tablespoons butter or	1 tablespoon red bell pepper,
margarine	chopped
3 cups Chicken Broth	2 tablespoons Parmesan cheese
4 tablespoons flour	Salt and pepper
2 cups milk	

Sauté onions in 6 tablespoons butter or margarine 10 minutes, or until onion is transparent, but not browned. Add Broth and cook, covered, 30 minutes. Strain, reserving Broth, and force onion through colander or food mill. Return pulp to Broth. In another saucepan, melt remaining 2 tablespoons butter or margarine and blend in flour. Gradually add milk and cook, stirring constantly, until thickened. Add egg yolk and cook 2 minutes more. Add milk mixture and chopped pepper to onion and Broth mixture. Season to taste with salt and pepper. Stir to blend well. Garnish bowls with Parmesan cheese. Makes 1^{1}/$_{2}$ quarts Soup.

PEANUT BUTTER SOUP

1 tablespoon cornstarch
4 cups milk
1 teaspoon onion juice
1 tablespoon celery, chopped

1 cup peanut butter
Salt and pepper
Peanuts

In the top of a double boiler combine most of milk, onion juice, celery and peanut butter. Combine the cornstarch with a little of the milk and cook over hot water until well blended, smooth and thickened. Force through a colander or food mill and season to taste with salt and pepper. Garnish each bowl with coarsely chopped peanuts. Makes 1 quart Soup.

CREAM OF POTATO-CHEESE SOUP

3 medium potatoes, chopped
1 medium onion, chopped
2 cups water
2 tablespoons butter or
    margarine
2 tablespoons flour

4 cups milk
1/2 cup American or cheddar
    cheese, shredded
Dash celery salt
Salt and pepper

Cook potato and onion in water until tender. Strain, reserving liquid. Force vegetables through a colander or food mill, then return pulp to liquid. In a saucepan, melt butter or margarine and blend in flour. Gradually add milk and cook until thickened. Add cheese and stir until cheese is melted. Add to potato mixture and stir well to blend. Season to taste with celery salt, salt and pepper. Makes 2 quarts Soup.

CREAM OF PEA SOUP

3 cups fresh peas (or a No. 2 can)
1 teaspoon onion, finely minced
1 cup water
3 tablespoons butter or margarine
3 tablespoons flour
3 cups milk
1/2 cup cream or evaporated milk
Salt and pepper

Cook peas and onion in 1 cup water. Strain, reserving liquid, and force peas through a colander or food mill. Return pulp to liquid. In another saucepan, melt butter and blend in flour. Gradually add milk and cook, stirring constantly, until thickened. Add cream or evaporated milk and stir into pea mixture. Season to taste with salt and pepper. Makes 1¹/₂ quarts Soup.

RIVEL SOUP

In Grandmother's day, rivels were called "Poor Man's Rice" because they often were substituted for the more expensive grain. Rivels are a simplified form of egg noodles.

2 quarts milk
1 cup flour
1/2 teaspoon salt
1 egg
Salt and pepper

Heat milk to scalding over hot water in top of double boiler. Meanwhile, add mixed flour and salt gradually to egg and beat with fork or rub with the fingers until small "rivels" the size of cherry seeds form. Drop a few at a time into hot milk and keep milk just below boiling point 3 to 5 minutes. Season to taste with salt and pepper. Makes 2 quarts Soup.

CREAM OF SPINACH SOUP

1-1/2 cups finely chopped
    spinach, cooked
   4 cups milk
   2 tablespoons butter or
    margarine

1/4 teaspoon lemon peel,
   grated
  1 tablespoon cornstarch
  1 tablespoon cold water
  Salt and pepper

Heat the spinach with the milk, butter or margarine and lemon peel. In a cup, blend the cornstarch with the cold water, then add to the soup. Stir and simmer 5 minutes, until slightly thickened. Season to taste with salt and pepper. Makes 1 quart Soup.

CREAM OF TOMATO SOUP

3-1/2 cups raw tomatoes,
   chopped
  2 teaspoons sugar
  2 slices onion
  5 whole cloves
  5 whole peppercorns
  3 sprigs parsley
  1 bay leaf

  3 tablespoons butter or
   margarine
  3 tablespoons flour
  3 cups milk
1/2 cup cream or evaporated
   milk
  Salt and pepper

Combine tomatoes, sugar and onion slices. Tie cloves, peppercorns, parsley and bay leaf in a small piece of cheesecloth and add. Simmer over low heat 15 minutes. Remove cheesecloth bag. Force tomatoes through a colander or food mill and add enough water to make 2 cups purée. Keep hot. Meanwhile, melt butter or margarine in a saucepan and blend in flour. Gradually add milk and cook until thickened, stirring constantly. Add cream or evaporated milk and heat to boiling. With both liquids hot (to keep milk from curdling) add tomato purée to the white sauce gradually, stirring constantly. Season to taste with salt and pepper. Makes 1 quart Soup.

CREAM OF SQUASH SOUP

2 slices onion	1 bay leaf
3 tablespoons butter or margarine	2 cups cooked, strained winter squash
3 tablespoons flour	Salt and pepper
4 cups milk	1/2 cup cream

Sauté onion in butter or margarine over low heat until transparent. Blend in flour and gradually add milk and bay leaf. Cook, stirring constantly, until thickened. Remove bay leaf. Add squash and force through a colander or food mill. Season with salt and pepper. Add cream and re-heat. Makes 1^1/$_2$ quarts Soup.

CREAM OF TURNIP SOUP

4 cups milk	margarine
1 medium onion, whole	1 tablespoon flour
4 turnips, grated	Salt and pepper
2 tablespoons butter or	2 tablespoons parsley, chopped

Heat milk in double boiler with whole onion. Add grated turnip and cook 10 to 15 minutes, or until turnip is soft. Remove onion and discard. In another saucepan, melt butter or margarine and blend in flour. Add enough of the hot milk mixture to make a smooth paste. Add to soup and blend well. Cook 5 minutes until smooth and creamy. Season to taste with salt and pepper. Garnish with chopped parsley. Makes 1 quart Soup.

CREAM OF VEGETABLE SOUP

3 medium potatoes, chopped
2 ribs celery, chopped
1 medium onion, chopped
1/8 teaspoon dried sage, crumbled
1 bay leaf
2 cups asparagus, cut up

4 cups water
2 tablespoons butter or margarine
2 tablespoons flour
2 cups milk
Salt and pepper

Cook potatoes, celery, onion, sage, bay leaf and asparagus in 4 cups water until vegetables are tender. Force through a colander or food mill. In another saucepan, melt butter or margarine and blend in flour. Gradually add milk and cook until thickened, stirring constantly. Add to vegetable mixture, stirring well to blend. Season to taste with salt and pepper. Makes 1¹/₂ quarts Soup.

VINEGAR SOUP

2 cups potatoes, sliced
2 quarts water
4 tablespoons butter or margarine
3 tablespoons flour

2 cups cream or evaporated milk
Salt and pepper
1/2 cup vinegar

Cook potatoes in the water until tender. Meanwhile, in another saucepan, melt butter or margarine and blend in the flour. Gradually add 1 cup potato water and cook, stirring constantly, until smooth. Add to soup kettle. Heat cream or evaporated milk to scalding and add. Season to taste with salt and pepper. Just before serving, stir in vinegar. Makes 2¹/₂ quarts Soup.

Budget Soups

There's no need to skimp on flavor or good nutrition just because the food budget is low.

These soup recipes make the most of leftovers and low-cost cuts of meats and small amounts of variety meats. Many of them utilize broths for flavor, instead of meat.

The next time the budget needs help, try one of the following recipes. Some of them are sure to become family favorites, on the first of the month, too.

BEANY-WIENY SOUP

1-3/4 cups dried pea beans	2 sprigs parsley
2 quarts cold water	1/4 teaspoon dried marjoram
2 quarts hot water	2 cups tomatoes
1 teaspoon salt	1 small onion, whole
1 clove garlic, minced	6 whole cloves
8 to 10 peppercorns	Salt and pepper
1 bay leaf	4 wieners, sliced in rings

Soak beans overnight in the cold water. In the morning, drain. Add the hot water and salt. Tie garlic, peppercorns, bay leaf, parsley and marjoram in a piece of cheesecloth. Set aside. Put beans in soup kettle and add tomatoes and whole onion which has cloves firmly imbedded in it. Simmer over low heat 2 or 3 hours, until beans are tender, adding cheesecloth bag last 30 minutes. Remove spice bag and onion and discard. Season to taste with salt and pepper. Garnish bowls and wiener slices. Makes $1^{1}/_{2}$ quarts Soup.

HAM AND CABBAGE SOUP

Leftover ham bone
(or 2 smoked ham hocks)
2 quarts cold water
10 peppercorns
4 whole cloves
1 clove garlic

Sprig parsley
3 medium potatoes, sliced
3 carrots, sliced
1 small head cabbage, shredded
Salt

Cover ham bone with the water. Add peppercorns, cloves, garlic and parsley. Cover and simmer 2 to 3 hours. Strain broth into clean kettle and cut meat from bone and add meat back to soup. Add potatoes and carrots and simmer 30 minutes. Add cabbage and cook 10 minutes longer. Season to taste with salt. Makes $1^{1}/_{2}$ quarts Soup.

HAMBURGER-VEGETABLE SOUP

1/2 pound lean ground beef
1 small onion, chopped
1 teaspoon salt
1 clove garlic, chopped
2 quarts Beef Broth
2 cups fresh or canned
   tomatoes

1/2 cup celery, sliced
1/2 cup fresh or frozen peas
1/2 cup fresh or canned green
   beans, cut up
1 cup carrots, chopped
1 cup cabbage, shredded
Salt and pepper

Combine ground beef, onion, salt and garlic. Form into 1-inch balls and pan fry without adding fat until browned on all sides. Add to Beef Broth and tomatoes and simmer 30 minutes. Add celery, peas, beans and carrots and cook 15 minutes, covered. Add cabbage and cook 15 minutes longer. Season to taste with salt and pepper. Makes 2 quarts Soup.

JERUSALEM ARTICHOKE SOUP

1/2 pound lean ham, cut in strips	4 pounds Jerusalem artichokes, cut in thin slices
3 tablespoons butter or margarine	2-1/2 quarts White Stock or Chicken Broth
1/2 rib celery, chopped	2 cups milk
1 turnip, chopped	2 teaspoons sugar
1 medium onion, chopped	Salt and pepper

Sauté the ham in the butter or margarine 15 minutes over low heat, stirring frequently to keep from sticking. Place the ham, celery, turnip, onion and artichokes in the soup kettle. Add Stock or Broth, cover and simmer 1 hour, or until vegetables are soft. Stir well or mash with a potato masher to thicken stock. Add milk and season to taste with sugar, pepper and salt. Makes 3 quarts Soup.

CREAM OF LEFTOVER SOUP

1 rib celery, sliced
1 small onion, chopped
4 tablespoons butter or
  margarine
3 tablespoons flour
2 cups Chicken Broth
  Pinch dried sage

1 bay leaf
4 cups leftover cooked vegetables
  (combination of carrots, peas,
  green or any other beans)
2 cups milk
  Salt and pepper

Sauté celery and onion in butter or margarine until onion is
transparent but not browned. Blend in flour and gradually add
Chicken Broth. Cook, stirring constantly, until thickened.
Lower heat, cover and cook 10 minutes. Add sage and bay leaf
and cook 5 minutes more. Remove bay leaf and add vegetables
and milk. Heat and season to taste with salt and pepper. Makes
2 quarts Soup.

LOW-COST MINESTRONE

1 cup dry Navy beans
2 quarts cold water
2 quarts boiling water
1/4 pound lean bacon, diced
1 small onion, chopped
1 clove garlic, chopped
1 cup canned tomatoes

1/2 cup turnip, chopped
1/2 cup carrot, chopped
1 cup cabbage, shredded
1 cup cooked macaroni
  Salt and pepper
3/4 cup Parmesan cheese

Soak beans overnight in the cold water to cover. Drain and add
2 quarts boiling water. Cover and simmer 2 hours, until tender. Meanwhile, cook bacon in skillet until crisp. Remove bacon, crumble and add to beans. Sauté onion and garlic in bacon
fat. Add to beans. Add tomatoes, turnip and carrots and sim-

mer 30 minutes. Add cabbage and simmer 10 minutes longer. Add cooked macaroni and season to taste with salt and pepper. Top bowls with Parmesan cheese. Makes 2 quarts Soup.

POTATO SOUP

3 medium potatoes, chopped
1 small onion, chopped
3 ribs celery, sliced
1 small carrot, grated
1 quart water
3 tablespoons butter

2 tablespoons flour
1 cup milk
1 cup evaporated milk
  Salt and pepper
  Paprika

Cook potatoes, onion, celery and carrot in the water until tender. Meanwhile, in another pan, melt butter and blend in flour. Gradually add milk and cook, stirring constantly, until thickened. Add to soup. Add evaporated milk. Season to taste with salt and pepper. Garnish bowls with paprika. Makes 2 quarts Soup.

LOW-COST PEPPER POT

2 tablespoons butter or
    margarine
1 medium onion, chopped
2 green peppers, chopped
1 rib celery, chopped
1/2 pound fresh or pickled tripe,
    cut in small pieces
2 quarts Beef Broth
10 peppercorns

1 bay leaf
1 teaspoon powdered thyme
1/2 cup carrots, chopped
1/4 cup spaghetti, broken in
    1-inch pieces
2 medium potatoes, chopped
1 cup fresh or canned tomatoes
    Salt and pepper

Melt butter in soup kettle. Sauté onion, pepper, celery and tripe 10 minutes, stirring frequently. Add Beef Broth. Tie peppercorns, bay leaf and thyme in a piece of cheesecloth and add. Cover and simmer 45 minutes. Remove cheesecloth bag, add carrots, spaghetti, potatoes and tomatoes. Cover and simmer 30 minutes longer. Season to taste with salt and pepper. Makes 2 quarts Soup.

QUICK PEA SOUP

4 cups (2 No. 2 cans)
    green peas
1 teaspoon onion, chopped
1/2 cup broth from boiled ham
2 cups milk

1 cup leftover ham, chopped
2 tablespoons flour
2 tablespoons cold water
    Salt and pepper

Put peas, the water in which they were canned, onion, ham broth and milk in blender. Blend 2 minutes. Pour into pan with ham and heat to simmering. Combine flour and water to make a paste. Gradually add to soup and cook, stirring, until thickened. Season to taste with salt and pepper. Makes 1^1/$_2$ quarts Soup.

PRINCE OF WALES SOUP

8 turnips   Salt and pepper
2 quarts White Stock   3 slices bread

Peel turnips and use ball cutter to cut them in marble-size pieces. Reserve scraps to chop and use in other soups. Simmer turnip balls in the White Stock until tender. Meanwhile, cut the bread into tiny circles with the center of a doughnut cutter. Season soup to taste with salt and pepper. Float circles of bread on each bowl of soup. Makes 2 quarts Soup.

SOUP MAIGRE

An old French recipe, the title means literally, "Soup of the Poor."

2 tablespoons butter or   2 quarts water
  margarine   2 tablespoons uncooked rice
1 onion, chopped   2 tablespoons butter or
1 carrot, chopped   margarine
3 ribs celery, sliced   2 tablespoons flour
2 tomatoes, peeled and chopped   Salt and pepper
2 bay leaves

Melt butter or margarine in soup kettle. Add onion, and carrot and cook over low heat, stirring constantly, until onion is transparent but not browned. Add the celery, tomatoes, bay leaves, water and rice. Cover and simmer over low heat until vegetables are tender. In another pan, melt the other 2 tablespoons butter or margarine and blend in flour. Add 1 cup of the soup stock and cook, stirring, until thickened. Add to soup and cook 10 minutes. Remove bay leaves and season to taste with salt and pepper. Makes 2 quarts Soup.

Fish and Shellfish Soups

If fish and shellfish are plentiful in your area, these soups can be a source of good protein at low cost. But even if you live inland, where they are more costly, a few of the following recipes can be made with the less expensive canned or frozen fish and oysters.

And, if you're a real fish enthusiast, you'll want to try the Bouillabaisse or the Green Turtle Soup regardless of cost. They're worth it.

A heartier type, such as Okra-Oyster Soup, may be served with a green salad and with fruit as a one-dish family meal. Serve Lobster Soup as the first course of a very special company dinner.

BOUILLABAISSE

Bouillabaisse is a rich, delicious combination of seafood and vegetables, seasoned with herbs and wine. Almost any combination of seafood will do, so don't hesitate to vary the kinds and amounts of fish and shellfish according to your taste and their availability in your area.

24 clams, mussels or oysters
 2 cups boiling water
 2 pounds haddock or perch
 4 cups boiling water
 2 cups shelled, deveined
   shrimp
Cooked meat from 1 lobster
   (about 1 cup)
 1 cup cooked crabmeat
1/2 cup cooking oil
 6 tomatoes, chopped
 1 tablespoon onion, finely
   chopped

 1 tablespoon celery, finely
   chopped
 1 teaspoon garlic, finely
   chopped
 1 teaspoon powdered sage
 1 teaspoon powdered thyme
 1 teaspoon saffron
 2 bay leaves
 1 teaspoon paprika
   Dash cayenne
 1 cup cooking sherry
   Salt and pepper
 1 lemon, thinly sliced
 1 tablespoon parsley, chopped

Steam the clams, mussels or oysters 2 minutes, using the 2 cups boiling water. Remove and set aside meat from shells, pouring the liquor from the shells into the soup kettle. Remove bones from the haddock or perch and place the meat in the soup kettle with the 4 cups boiling water. Cover and simmer 10 minutes. Drain, reserving the fish stock. Heat oil in a large kettle. Combine all fish and shellfish meats, tomatoes, onion, celery, garlic, sage, thyme, saffron, bay leaves, paprika and cayenne and add to hot oil. Simmer, stirring constantly, 10 minutes. Add fish stock and sherry and cook over very low heat another 30 minutes. Remove bay leaves. Season to taste with salt and pepper and garnish each bowl with thin lemon slices and chopped parsley. Makes 2$^{1}/_{2}$ quarts Bouillabaisse.

CATFISH SOUP

6 small, cleaned, skinned
  catfish
1-1/2 pounds ham, cut in 1-inch
  cubes
  Sprig parsley
  Sprig marjoram
3 ribs celery

2 quarts water
4 tablespoons butter or
  margarine
4 tablespoons flour
4 cups milk
2 egg yolks, slightly beaten
  Salt and pepper

Place catfish, ham, parsley, marjoram and celery in soup kettle. Cover with the 2 quarts water and simmer over low heat until ham and catfish are tender but not overcooked. Strain broth into another pan and remove bones from fish. Return fish and ham to the broth. Discard bones and cooked herbs. Re-heat broth. In another saucepan, melt butter or margarine, blend in flour and gradually add milk. Cook, stirring constantly, until thickened. Add egg yolks and cook 2 minutes more over low heat. Combine with fish-ham mixture, stirring well to blend. Season to taste with salt and pepper. Makes $2^1/2$ quarts Soup.

CLAM SOUP

24 clams
4 cups boiling water
2 cups water
  Dash of cayenne

4 cups milk
2 tablespoons butter or
  margarine
  Salt and pepper

Place clams in large pan and pour 4 cups boiling water over them. As they begin to open, remove the clams quickly and re-serve, pouring the liquor in them into the soup kettle. Add the 2 cups water to kettle. Add cayenne and the clams. Simmer, covered, 30 minutes. Add the milk and butter or margarine and season to taste with salt and pepper. Makes $1^1/2$ quarts Soup.

CRAB SOUP

1 cup cooked or canned crab meat
2 hard-cooked eggs, chopped
3 cups light cream or partially diluted evaporated milk
1/8 teaspoon dry mustard
1/8 teaspoon ground mace
4 teaspoons butter or margarine
Salt and pepper
4 thin slices lemon
1 tablespoon parsley, chopped

Flake the crabmeat and remove any bits of shell. Combine with the egg, cream or milk, mustard and mace. Heat it in a double boiler until quite hot, but not boiling. Add the butter or margarine and stir to mix well. Season to taste with salt and pepper. Garnish each bowl with a slice of lemon and chopped parsley. Makes 1 quart Soup.

GREEN TURTLE SOUP

Green turtle meat sometimes is available in specialty sections of large supermarkets. Any cooked or canned turtle meat, also, may be substituted in this recipe.

2 cups green turtle meat	Sprig of sage
6 cups Brown Stock	3 tablespoons butter or margarine
4 whole cloves	
4 peppercorns	1 small onion, chopped
1 bay leaf	3 tablespoons flour
1 blade (or 1/2 tsp. ground) mace	Salt
Sprig of savory	Dash of cayenne
Sprig of marjoram	1/4 cup cooking sherry
Sprig of thyme	1 lemon, sliced

Cut turtle meat into 1/2-inch cubes. Put into soup kettle and add 4 cups of the Brown Stock. Tie cloves, peppercorns, bay leaf, mace, savory, marjoram, thyme and sage in a small piece of cheesecloth. Add to soup kettle and cover. Cook 30 minutes over low heat. Meanwhile, in another saucepan, melt butter and add onion. Sauté over low heat until onion is transparent. Blend in flour and gradually add remaining 2 cups Brown Stock. Cook, stirring constantly, until thickened. Add to turtle mixture and season to taste with salt and cayenne. Remove cheesecloth bag and add sherry. Stir well. Garnish each bowl with a slice of lemon. Makes 2 quarts Soup.

LOBSTER SOUP

3 large lobsters (1 1/2 to
  2 pounds each)
2 anchovies (or smoked fillets)
1 small onion, chopped
  Sprig thyme
  Sprig marjoram
  Sprig parsley
1 strip lemon peel
1/8 teaspoon nutmeg

4 cups water
2 tablespoons butter or
  margarine
1 teaspoon flour
2 cups milk
2 cups cream or evaporated
  milk
  Salt and pepper

Steam the lobsters and pick out as much meat as possible. Add to the soup kettle with the anchovies. Tie the onion, herbs and lemon peel in a piece of cheesecloth and add. Add the 4 cups water. Cover and simmer over low heat 30 minutes. Meanwhile, in another pan, melt the butter or margarine and blend in the flour. Gradually add the milk and cook, stirring constantly, until slightly thickened. Add slowly to the soup kettle. Add the cream or evaporated milk. Season to taste with salt and pepper. Makes 2 quarts Soup.

Many of the recipes in this book call for fresh herbs, but if these are not available, dried herbs may be substituted. Dried herbs, however, may have to be placed in a muslin bag if the recipe calls for the herbs later to be removed.

Remember that dried herbs are much stronger flavored than fresh, and you may need to experiment to find out the amount your family prefers. Begin with 1/4 to 1/2 teaspoon of dried herb leaves to replace a fresh sprig.

OKRA-OYSTER SOUP

2 small onions, chopped
2 tablespoons butter or
  margarine
3 tablespoons uncooked rice
2 cups tomatoes, fresh or canned
1 red bell pepper, chopped

2 quarts boiling water
  Oyster liquor
2 cups fresh okra, sliced
2 dozen oysters
  Salt and pepper

Sauté the chopped onions in the butter or margarine over low heat until onion is transparent but not browned. Pour into the soup kettle and add rice, tomatoes, sweet pepper, water and oyster liquor. Simmer over low heat 30 minutes. Add the okra and shelled oysters and heat almost to boiling. Season to taste with salt and pepper. Makes 3 quarts Soup.

OYSTER STEW

6 dozen oysters
  Oyster liquor
2 quarts White Stock
2 tablespoons butter or
  margarine

2 tablespoons flour
1 cup cream
  Salt and cayenne

Scald the shelled oysters in their own liquor. Heat 6 cups of the White Stock to boiling and add. Simmer 30 minutes. Meanwhile, in another saucepan, melt the butter or margarine, and blend in the flour. Gradually add the 2 remaining cups White Stock and cook until thickened, stirring constantly. Add to oyster mixture and stir well. Add cream and season to taste with salt and cayenne. Makes 3 quarts Stew.

SALMON SOUP

4 tablespoons butter or margarine
2 quarts milk

2 cups canned red or pink salmon, flaked
Salt and pepper

Brown butter lightly in soup kettle. Add milk and salmon. Heat just to simmering and cook gently 5 minutes. Season to taste with salt and pepper. Makes $2^1/2$ quarts Soup.

TURTLE SOUP

Sprig thyme
1 bay leaf
Sprig parsley
2 quarts Chicken Broth
1-1/2 pounds cooked or canned turtle meat, cubed

1/2 pound fresh or canned mushrooms, chopped
1 tablespoon cornstarch
1 tablespoon cold water
Salt and pepper
2 hard-cooked eggs, sliced
1 lemon, thinly sliced

Gently simmer the thyme, bay leaf and parsley in the Chicken Broth 10 minutes. Strain. Add cooked turtle meat and mushrooms. Slowly heat to simmering again. Meanwhile, add the cornstarch to the cold water and stir to a thin paste. Stir into the broth and cook, stirring, until slightly thickened. Season to taste with salt and pepper. Put 2 egg slices in each bowl and pour soup over. Garnish with a slice of lemon. Makes $2^1/2$ quarts Soup.

VEGETABLE-OYSTER SOUP

1 pint small shelled oysters
   Oyster liquor
4 tablespoons butter or
   margarine
2 medium carrots, chopped
1 rib celery, chopped

4 cups milk
1 cup light cream or evaporated
   milk
   Salt and pepper
   Sprig parsley, chopped

Gently simmer oysters in their own liquor until the edges begin to curl, about 5 minutes. Meanwhile, in another saucepan, melt butter or margarine and add carrots and celery. Cover and cook over low heat until tender. Stir occasionally and do not allow to brown. Add vegetables to cooked oysters and add milk and cream or evaporated milk. Season to taste with salt and pepper. Garnish each bowl with chopped parsley. Makes $1^1/2$ quarts Soup.

Chowders

Chowders are thick, almost stew-like soups made of fish or meat and vegetables. Potatoes and milk usually are main ingredients.

Serve meat and fish chowders for informal dinners in heavy bowls with homemade breads. Vegetable chowders make inexpensive yet nourishing main dishes for lunch, also.

Remember, chowders are not suitable for canning or freezing.

CELERY CHOWDER

1 small onion, chopped
1 tablespoon butter or margarine
3 cups celery, chopped
1 cup potatoes, chopped

2 cups water
4 cups milk
2 hard-cooked eggs, chopped
Salt and pepper

Sauté onion in butter or margarine in soup kettle. Add celery, potatoes and water. Cover and cook over low heat until tender. Add milk and chopped eggs and season to taste with salt and pepper. Makes 2 quarts Chowder.

CHEESE CHOWDER

1 medium onion, chopped
1/2 cup celery, chopped
2 tablespoons butter or
  margarine
2 cups potatoes, chopped
2 cups water
1 bay leaf
1/2 teaspoon powdered basil

2 cups canned cream-style
  corn
1-1/2 cups milk
1 cup fresh or canned
  tomatoes, chopped
1/2 cup grated process cheese
Salt and pepper
Sprig parsley

Sauté onion and celery in butter or margarine until onion is transparent but not browned. Add potatoes and water. Tie bay leaf and basil in a piece of cheesecloth and add. Cover and cook until potatoes are tender. Remove cheesecloth bag and add corn, milk, tomatoes and cheese. Heat, stirring constantly, until cheese is melted. Season to taste with salt and pepper and garnish each bowl with chopped parsley. Makes 1½ quarts Chowder.

CHICKEN CHOWDER

1 tablespoon onion, chopped
3 tablespoons butter or
  margarine
1 quart Chicken Broth
1 quart milk

1 cup leftover cooked chicken,
  cut in small pieces
2 cups cooked potato, chopped
2 tablespoons flour
Salt and pepper

Sauté the onion in 1 tablespoon of the butter or margarine until transparent but not browned. Add broth, milk, chicken and potato and simmer 5 minutes. Meanwhile, melt remaining 2 tablespoons butter and blend in flour. Gradually add 1 cup of the soup and cook until thickened. Add back to soup and stir well. Season to taste with salt and pepper. Makes 2 quarts Chowder.

CLAM CHOWDER

24 clams in the shell
 4 quarts boiling water
2-inch cube of salt pork
 1 small onion, chopped
 4 medium potatoes, sliced thin

2 quarts water
1 quart milk
1 tablespoon butter or
  margarine
Salt and pepper

Cover clams with the boiling water. As quickly as the shells open, remove the clams, adding the liquor inside them to the soup kettle. Remove the thin skin from the clams and cut off all the black end and discard. Chop the tough parts and leave the soft part whole. In another pan, fry the salt pork and onion until the onion is transparent. Add the salt pork and onion, potatoes and 2 quarts water to the soup kettle. Cover and cook over low heat until potatoes are tender. Add clams, milk and butter or margarine. Heat through. Season to taste with salt and pepper. Makes 3 quarts Chowder.

CODFISH CHOWDER

2 cups salt codfish, shredded
2 cups cold water
3 cups potato, cut in cubes
3 cups boiling water
2 small onions, chopped
2 tablespoons butter or
   margarine

4 tablespoons butter or
   margarine
2 tablespoons flour
1 cup cream or evaporated milk
   Dash of cayenne
   Salt and pepper
8 crackers, buttered

Soak codfish in the cold water one hour. Drain, discarding water. Cook cubed potatoes 10 minutes in the 3 cups boiling water. Meanwhile, sauté onion in 2 tablespoons butter or margarine until onion is transparent but not browned. Combine drained codfish, potatoes, potato water and onion in soup kettle. Cover and cook until potatoes are soft. In another saucepan, melt the other 4 tablespoons butter or margarine and blend in flour. Gradually add cream or evaporated milk and cook until thickened. Add to soup kettle. Season to taste with salt and pepper and cayenne. Garnish each bowl with buttered crackers. Makes 1 quart Chowder.

CONEY ISLAND CHOWDER

3 pounds fresh fish (perch,
   haddock, cod, catfish, etc.)
2 quarts boiling water
1/4 pound salt pork
1 small onion, chopped
1/2 teaspoon thyme
1/2 teaspoon summer savory
6 whole cloves
1 bay leaf

   Sprig parsley
4 medium potatoes, sliced
3 cups tomato juice
3 tablespoons butter or
   margarine
3 tablespoons flour
   Salt and pepper
2/3 cup cracker crumbs

Skin and fillet the fish. Cut meat in 2-inch pieces and set aside. Cover the heads, body bones and trimmings with the 2 quarts boiling water and simmer 30 minutes. Strain and discard all but the broth. Cut the salt pork into bits and cook out the fat slowly to avoid browning. In this fat sauté the chopped onion over low heat until onion is transparent, but not browned. Add fat and onion to strained broth in the soup kettle. Tie thyme, savory, cloves, bay leaf and parsley in a piece of cheesecloth and add to the kettle. Add the potatoes and tomato juice. Simmer until potatoes are tender. In another saucepan, melt butter or margarine and blend in flour. Add 1 cup of the soup broth gradually and cook until thickened, stirring constantly. Add back to soup kettle. Remove spice bag and discard. Season to taste with salt and pepper. Makes 3 quarts Chowder.

CORN CHOWDER

1/4 pound salt pork	1 cup milk
1 onion, sliced	1 cup cream or evaporated
1 quart potatoes, sliced	milk
2 cups water	2 tablespoons butter or
1 quart fresh corn pulp (see	margarine
Cream of Corn recipe,	Salt and pepper
page 82)	

Cut the pork into small pieces and cook out the fat slowly. Add the sliced onion and cook until onion is transparent but not browned. Add potatoes and water and cook until potatoes are tender. Add corn and cook 5 minutes longer. Add milk, cream or evaporated milk and butter or margarine and heat to simmering. Season to taste with salt and pepper. Makes 2¹/₂ quarts Chowder.

CRAB CHOWDER

1 small onion, chopped	2 cups cooked crab meat
4 tablespoons butter or margarine	1 cup cream or evaporated milk
2 tablespoons flour	Salt and pepper
4 cups milk	Dash of cayenne

Sauté onion in butter or margarine until onion is transparent. Stir well to prevent browning. Blend in flour and gradually add milk. Cook, stirring constantly, over low heat until thickened. Add crab meat and cream or evaporated milk and season to taste with salt, cayenne and pepper. Makes 1^1/$_2$ quarts Chowder.

LOBSTER CHOWDER

1/4 pound salt pork, chopped	margarine
1 small onion, chopped	1-1/2 cups cream or evaporated milk
2 tablespoons flour	
4 cups milk	Salt and pepper
2 cups cooked lobster meat	Dash of cayenne
3 tablespoons butter or	

Fry pork to cook out fat. Add onion and sauté until onion is transparent. Blend in flour and gradually add milk. Cook over low heat, stirring constantly, until thickened. Add lobster meat and cook gently over low heat 10 to 15 minutes. Add butter and cream and season to taste with salt, cayenne and pepper. Makes 2 quarts Chowder.

FISH CHOWDER

1 tablespoon salt pork, diced	1 tablespoon butter or
1 small onion, chopped	margarine
1 medium potato, chopped	2 cups shredded salmon (or
1 cup tomato, chopped	other cooked fish)
2 cups Beef Broth	Salt and pepper

Fry pork to cook out fat. Add onion and sauté until transparent. Add potatoes, tomatoes, broth and butter or margarine. Cover and simmer until vegetables are tender. Add salmon and season to taste with salt and pepper. Makes 1 quart Chowder.

MANHATTAN CLAM CHOWDER

1 small onion, sliced	2 cups canned tomatoes
1 clove garlic, minced	1/8 teaspoon thyme
1/4 pound salt pork, chopped	2 cups fresh clams
1/4 cup celery, chopped	(20 to 24 clams)
1/4 cup carrots, chopped	Clam liquor
1 cup potatoes, chopped	Salt and pepper
3 cups water	

Over low heat, sauté onion, garlic and salt pork 5 minutes, stirring constantly. Add celery, carrots, potatoes, water, tomatoes and thyme. Cover and simmer 15 minutes, until potatoes are tender. If clams in shells are used, open shells as in Clam Chowder, page 109. Remove the tough parts from the clams and chop these fine. Add to the soup kettle. Leave the soft parts whole and add 2 to 3 minutes before serving. Season to taste with salt and pepper. Makes 2 quarts Chowder.

NEW ENGLAND FISH CHOWDER

1/4 pound salt pork, diced
 2 medium onions, chopped
 2 cups chopped potatoes
 2 cups boiling water
 2 cups clam meat and liquor
 2 pounds haddock

 2 tablespoons butter or
    margarine
 1 tablespoon flour
 4 cups milk
 1 cup cream or evaporated
    milk
    Salt and pepper

Fry salt pork until golden brown. Add onions and potatoes. Cover and cook over low heat until onions begin to turn light brown. Add the boiling water and cook until potatoes are tender. Add clams (see directions under Clam Chowder, page 109 if in shells) and fish which has been boned and cut into bite-size pieces. Simmer 10 minutes. Meanwhile, melt butter or margarine in another saucepan. Blend in flour and gradually add milk. Cook, stirring constantly, until thickened. Add to soup. Add cream or evaporated milk and season to taste with salt and pepper. Makes 2 quarts Chowder.

OKRA CHOWDER

1 medium onion, chopped
2 cups celery, chopped
1 green pepper, chopped
4 tablespoons butter or
   margarine
1 pound fresh okra, sliced thin

2 large tomatoes, peeled and
   sliced
1 teaspoon sugar
4 cups boiling water
   Salt and pepper

Sauté onion, celery and green pepper in butter or margarine over low heat 5 minutes. Add okra, tomatoes, sugar and water. Cover and simmer 30 minutes. Season to taste with salt and pepper. Makes 1 1/2 quarts Chowder.

ONION CHOWDER

2 cups onion, chopped
3 tablespoons butter or
  margarine
4 cups potatoes, diced

3 quarts boiling water
  Salt and pepper
  Sprig thyme, chopped
  Sprig parsley, chopped

Sauté onion in the butter or margarine over low heat until onion is transparent but not browned. Add potatoes and boiling water and cook, covered, until potatoes are tender. Season to taste with salt and pepper and garnish each bowl with chopped thyme and parsley. Makes 3½ quarts Chowder.

VEGETABLE CHOWDER

2 cups corn, fresh or canned
2 cups celery, chopped
1/2 green pepper, cut in thin
    strips
1 medium onion, thinly
  sliced
1 cup tomatoes, canned or
  fresh

2-1/2 cups cold water
    4 tablespoons butter or
      margarine
    3 tablespoons flour
    2 cups milk
      Salt and pepper
  1/2 cup pimiento

Simmer corn, celery, green pepper, onion and tomatoes in the water 30 minutes. Meanwhile, melt the butter or margarine in a saucepan and blend in flour. Gradually add milk and cook, stirring constantly, until thickened. Add to vegetable-water mixture. Season to taste with salt and pepper. Garnish each bowl with chopped pimiento. Makes 2 quarts Chowder.

OYSTER CHOWDER

1/4 pound salt pork, diced
  2 small onions, chopped
  2 cups potatoes, chopped
  2 cups water
  1 tablespoon butter or
    margarine

1 tablespoon flour
4 cups milk
1 pint oysters with liquor
  Salt and pepper

Fry salt pork until brown. Add onions, potatoes and the water and simmer until potatoes are tender. In another pan, melt butter and blend in flour. Gradually add milk and stir until thickened. Add to soup kettle. Add oysters and oyster liquor and cook 5 minutes. Season to taste with salt and pepper. Makes 2 quarts Chowder.

SHRIMP CHOWDER

2 cups potatoes, chopped
1 small onion, chopped
2 cups water
4 tablespoons butter or
   margarine

2 tablespoons flour
4 cups milk
2 cups cooked shrimp, cut up
1 cup cream or evaporated milk
  Salt and pepper

Cook potatoes and onion in the water until tender. Meanwhile in a saucepan, melt butter and blend in flour. Gradually add milk and cook, stirring constantly, until thickened. Add shrimp meat and simmer 5 minutes. Add cream or evaporated milk, and season to taste with salt and pepper. Makes 2 quarts Chowder.

Bisques

Bisques are elegant versions of cream soups. Slightly thickened clear broths, they are served with or without small bits of meat, and in tiny cups as appetizers before company dinners.

CLAM BISQUE

2 cups shelled clams
2 cups Chicken Broth
2 tablespoons onion, chopped
3 tablespoons butter or margarine
4 tablespoons flour

Clam liquor, strained
1 bay leaf
2 cups cream, heated
1 teaspoon Worcestershire sauce
Salt and pepper

Chop the tough parts of the clams as in Clam Chowder recipe, page 109 and add to the Chicken Broth in soup kettle, cooking 20 minutes. Leave soft parts whole and set aside. Meanwhile, in a saucepan, sauté onions in butter or margarine until onion is transparent but not browned. Blend in flour and gradually add clam liquor. Cook until smooth and thickened. Add bay leaf and soft clam parts and cook 5 minutes over low heat. Remove bay leaf and discard. Add onion mixture to soup kettle. Add heated cream and Worcestershire sauce and season to taste with salt and pepper. Makes $1^1/2$ quarts Bisque.

CHICKEN BISQUE

2 tablespoons butter or
  margarine
1-1/2 tablespoons flour
3 cups Chicken Broth
1 cup cooked chicken,
  chopped fine

1 cup milk, heated to
  scalding
Salt and pepper
Watercress, chopped

Melt butter or margarine and blend in flour. Gradually add Chicken Broth and chicken. Cook, stirring constantly, until thickened. Add the milk and season to taste with salt and pepper. Makes 1 quart Bisque.

CRAB BISQUE

3 tablespoons butter or
  margarine
1 medium onion, sliced
4 tablespoons flour
3 cups milk
1 cup Chicken Broth

1-1/2 cups cooked crab meat
Sprig parsley, chopped
1/2 cup cream or evaporated
  milk
Salt and pepper

Melt butter or margarine in a large saucepan. Sauté onion until transparent and golden brown. Blend in flour. Gradually add milk and Broth and cook, stirring constantly, until the mixture thickens. Add crabmeat and parsley and cook over low heat 10 minutes. Force through a colander or food mill and re-heat, adding cream or evaporated milk. Season to taste with salt and pepper. Makes 1 quart Bisque.

SHRIMP BISQUE

3 tablespoons butter or margarine
2 cups fresh shelled, de-veined shrimp, cut up
2 tablespoons onion, chopped
1 small carrot, chopped
1/2 celery rib, chopped

1/2 cup fresh or canned mushrooms, chopped
3 cups White Stock
  Salt and pepper
  Dash of cayenne
1 cup white wine

Melt butter or margarine in large saucepan. Add shrimps, onion, carrot, celery and mushrooms and White Stock. Cover and simmer over low heat 20 minutes. Force through a colander or food mill and season to taste with salt, pepper and cayenne. Stir in wine just before serving. Makes 1 quart Bisque.

TOMATO BISQUE

2-1/2 cups fresh or canned tomatoes
2 teaspoons sugar
1 small onion, chopped
3 tablespoons butter or margarine

1 bay leaf
  Sprig parsley
1 cup dry bread crumbs
4 cups milk
  Salt and pepper

Cook tomatoes with sugar 15 minutes. Sauté onion in butter or margarine and add. Add bay leaf and parsley and cook 5 minutes longer. Remove bay leaf. Force through a colander or food mill and put in soup kettle. In another saucepan, add bread crumbs to milk and heat to scalding. Force through colander or food mill and add to soup kettle. Stir well to blend. Season to taste with salt and pepper. Makes 1¹/₂ quarts Bisque.

OYSTER BISQUE

2 tablespoons butter or
  margarine
2 tablespoons flour
3 cups milk
  Oyster liquor
1/2 teaspoon paprika
1/8 teaspoon powdered nutmeg

1 pint shelled oysters
2 egg yolks, well beaten
1/4 cup cream or evaporated
  milk
  Salt and pepper
  Celery leaves, finely chopped

Melt the butter or margarine and blend in flour. Add milk and liquor drained from oysters, and cook, stirring constantly, until smooth and thickened. Add paprika, nutmeg and oysters which have been cut up with scissors. Put the soup over hot (not boiling) water and let stand 5 minutes. Meanwhile, beat egg yolks until thick and add cream or evaporated milk. Beat again. One tablespoon at a time, add 1/4 cup soup mixture to the eggs. Blend well and stir egg mixture into soup. Heat over hot water another 5 minutes. Garnish each bowl with finely chopped celery leaves. Makes 1 quart Bisque.

LOBSTER BISQUE

1 large live lobster (about
  2 pounds)
2 quarts boiling water
1 teaspoon salt
2 cups cold water

4 tablespoons butter or
  margarine
3 tablespoons flour
4 cups milk
  Salt and pepper
  Dash of cayenne

Plunge live lobster into boiling water to which salt has been added. Boil briskly 10 minutes. Remove lobster to cool and

discard water. To extract meat from lobster, split lengthwise, starting at the head. Remove stomach and intestinal vein. Extract the meat, chop and set aside. Crack claws and take out meat. Chop tender portion of claw meat and add to body meat. In the soup kettle, add cold water to body shell and tough end of claw meat, cut in pieces. Bring slowly to boil and cook 20 minutes. Drain, reserving liquid. Pick any remaining meat from shell and chop fine. Discard shell. In another pan, melt butter or margarine and blend in flour. Gradually add milk and cook, stirring constantly, until smooth and thickened. Add all chopped lobster meat to broth and re-heat to simmering. Add milk mixture and season to taste with salt, pepper and cayenne. Makes 1^{1}/$_{2}$ quarts Bisque.

Gumbos

Okra is the characteristic ingredient of Gumbo, a thick Creole dish which is thicker than most soups, but thinner than stews.

In the southern states, Gumbo is a flavorful way of using okra, one of the most plentiful vegetables in season. For these variations, fresh, frozen or canned okra may be used.

CHICKEN GUMBO

1 stewing chicken, cut up	1 cup fresh or frozen whole-kernel canned corn
1/4 cup chicken fat	
3/4 pound lean veal, cut in cubes	1 quart okra slices
1 small onion, sliced	Salt and pepper
7 cups boiling water	1/2 teaspoon filé powder or 1 bay leaf, crushed

Lightly brown the chicken and veal in chicken fat, adding a few pieces at a time. When all are browned, add onion slices. Cover and reduce heat and cook 10 minutes. Put all into soup kettle. Add water and simmer over low heat 2 hours, or until meats are tender. Add corn and okra and cook 20 minutes longer. Season to taste with salt and pepper. Just before serving, add filé powder, mix well and serve. Makes 3 quarts Gumbo.

BEEF GUMBO

2 pounds lean beef, cut in
   small pieces
1/2 pound fresh pork, cubed
4 tablespoons butter or
   margarine

1 quart fresh tomates, sliced
3 quarts hot water
2 quarts 1/2-inch okra slices
   Salt and pepper

Sauté the beef and pork in the butter or margarine until lightly browned. Cover and cook over low heat, stirring occasionally, until tender. Put into soup kettle. Add tomatoes and water and simmer 1 hour. Add okra and cook 20 minutes longer. Season to taste with salt and pepper. Makes 3¹/₂ quarts Gumbo.

CHICKEN-OYSTER GUMBO

1 stewing chicken, cut up
1/4 cup butter or margarine
1/4 cup onion, chopped
1 tablespoon red bell pepper,
   chopped
4 quarts water
1 quart shelled oysters,
   with liquor

1 quart okra, sliced
2 tablespoons butter or
   margarine
2 tablespoons flour
   Salt and pepper
1 cup cooked rice

Sauté chicken pieces in butter or margarine. Remove chicken to soup kettle and sauté onion and bell pepper in butter. Cover and cook 10 minutes over low heat. Put into soup kettle. Add water and simmer 2 hours. Add oysters and okra and cook over low heat 20 minutes until okra is just done and oysters' edges curl. Meanwhile, in another pan, melt 2 tablespoons butter or margarine and blend in flour. Gradually add 2 cups of the soup broth and cook until thickened. Add back to soup kettle. Season to taste with salt and pepper. Garnish each bowl with rice. Makes 3¹/₂ quarts Gumbo.

CRAB GUMBO

1 cup salt pork, cubed	1 tablespoon red bell pepper, chopped
4 cups cooked or canned crab meat	4 tablespoons butter or margarine
1/4 cup onion, chopped	4 tablespoons flour
1 clove garlic, minced	1 cup cream or evaporated milk
1 quart okra slices	
2 quarts water	Salt and pepper
1 bay leaf	1 cup rice, cooked
Sprig thyme	

Cook the salt pork in a skillet 5 minutes. Add crab meat and sauté to golden brown. Remove crab meat to kettle. Add onion, garlic and okra to skillet and sauté until golden. Add to crab meat and cover with water. Tie bay leaf and thyme in a piece of cheesecloth and add. Add bell pepper and simmer over low heat 45 minutes. Meanwhile, in another saucepan, melt butter or margarine and blend in flour. Gradually add 1 cup of the soup stock and cook until thickened. Return to soup. Remove cheesecloth bag. Add cream or evaporated milk. Season to taste with salt and pepper and garnish with cooked rice. Makes 3 quarts Gumbo.

HAM GUMBO

1 small onion, chopped	3 large tomatoes, peeled
1/2 pod hot red pepper, chopped	and quartered
	1 bay leaf
1-1/2 quarts okra, sliced	Sprig thyme
2 tablespoons butter or margarine	Sprig parsley
	Salt and pepper
2 quarts Chicken Broth	Hot cooked rice
1 pound cooked ham, cubed	

In a heavy skillet, sauté the onion, red pepper and okra in butter or margarine until lightly browned. Cover, lower heat and cook 30 minutes, stirring occasionally to keep from sticking. Add broth, ham and tomatoes. Tie bay leaf, thyme and parsley in a piece of cheesecloth. Add and simmer 30 minutes. Remove cheesecloth bag. Season to taste with salt and pepper. Garnish each bowl with hot cooked rice. Makes 2$^1/_2$ quarts Gumbo.

Chili Con Carne

It's a well-known fact among chili lovers that you can tell where people come from by the way they like their chili.

In Texas, where chili has been the mainstay of the poor since the late 1700s, chili consists of tiny chunks of beef in a hot brown sauce—no onions, no tomatoes, no vegetables of any kind. Texans claim chili as a heritage of their robust past, when beef—and little else—was plentiful. Pinto beans often are served as an accompaniment but not as part of the dish.

Following are some regional recipes for chili, one of the most American dishes and one of the best cold weather budget stretchers yet devised:

CALIFORNIA CHILI

1 pound dry pinto beans	Salt
2 cups cold water	3 pounds cubed or coarsely
1/4 cup onion, chopped	ground beef
2 cloves garlic, minced	1 quart canned tomatoes
3 tablespoons shortening	1 teaspoon ground oregano
1/4 cup chili powder	Salt
1 tablespoon flour	

Soak beans overnight in the water. Cook until tender in soaking water, adding more if necessary. Brown onion and garlic in shortening. Blend in chili powder mixed with flour. Add to onion, garlic, beans and meat. Cover and cook 1 hour. Add tomatoes and oregano. Cover and simmer 1¹/₂ hours longer. Add salt to taste. Makes 1¹/₂ quarts Chili.

DEEP SOUTH CHILI

1-1/3 cups dry kidney beans
   1 quart water
   1 onion, chopped
   2 tablespoons shortening
   1 clove garlic, minced
   1 medium green pepper, chopped

   3 pounds ground beef
   1 pound fresh pork, ground
   1 quart fresh or canned tomatoes
   1 tablespoon chili powder
   1 tablespoon sugar
   Salt and pepper

Soak beans overnight in water to cover. Drain. Cover with 1 quart fresh water and simmer until tender. Brown onion slightly in hot shortening in a heavy skillet. Add garlic and green pepper. Add ground beef and pork and cook until lightly browned. Stir in tomatoes, chili powder and sugar. Simmer 2 hours. Add cooked beans. Season to taste with salt and pepper. Makes 1¹/₂ quarts Chili.

MIDWESTERN CHILI

2 pounds ground beef
1 medium onion, chopped
1 green pepper, chopped
2 tablespoons chili powder

1 rib celery, chopped
3 cups tomato juice
  Salt and pepper
2 cups cooked kidney beans

In a heavy skillet, sprinkle ground beef, onion and green pepper with chili powder. Cook until vegetables are tender, but not browned. Add celery and tomato juice, cover and cook 2 hours over low heat. Season to taste with salt and pepper. Add kidney beans and simmer 20 minutes longer. Makes 1¹/₂ quarts Chili.

NEW ENGLAND CHILI

2 tablespoons shortening	2 cans (10-3/4 oz. size)
1/2 cup onion, chopped	condensed tomato soup
1 clove garlic, minced	2 soup cans water
1 pound ground beef	1 can red kidney beans
1 tablespoon chili powder	Salt and pepper
1/4 teaspoon cayenne	

Melt shortening in skillet. Add onions, garlic and beef. Brown. Add seasonings, soup, water and kidney beans. Cover and simmer 30 minutes, stirring occasionally. Season to taste with salt and pepper. Makes 1¹/₂ quarts Chili.

CHILI PEPPERS

Chili peppers, the ingredient for which Chili Con Carne was named and from which it derives its distinctive flavor, are grown on a small, compact plant much like the bell pepper and pimiento plants.

There are two varieties of chilies—hot and mild. A blend of both hot and mild chilies, dried, then ground to a powder, is the main ingredient of commercial chili powder, which also includes ground cumin seed and oregano.

Some of the recipes in this section use only commercially prepared chili powder to obtain the chili flavor. Others, such as Texas Chili (page 131) call for a combination of chili powder, plus additional cumin and oregano. One recipe—New Mexico Chili (page 129)—derives its flavor from whole, mild chili peppers, ground oregano, whole cumin seed and hot, red chilies cut in very thin strips. Garbanzo-Noodle Soup (page 40) uses hot chili pepper.

Season with hot chilies carefully, adjusting the amount according to your taste. Even more than with most seasonings, just the right amount of chili peppers is delicious, but too much can ruin a dish.

NEW MEXICO CHILI

1/4 cup cooking oil
  2 pounds lean beef, pork or
    lamb, cubed
  2 tablespoons flour
  1 medium onion, chopped
  2 cloves garlic, minced
  6 to 8 mild chilies (chili
    peppers), seeds removed

  1 teaspoon oregano
1/4 teaspoon cumin seed, whole
  2 small hot chili peppers
  2 cups Brown Stock
    Salt
    Cooked pinto beans

Heat oil in heavy skillet. Add meat. Brown lightly over moderate heat. Push meat to one side of skillet. Mix flour, onion and garlic and add to skillet. Cook until onions are lightly browned. Add Brown Stock. Remove stems and seeds from chili pods and red peppers. Cut in very thin strips with scissors. Add to meat —onion. Add oregano and cumin seed and Brown Stock. Cover tightly and simmer over low heat until meat is tender, about 2 hours. Season to taste with salt. Serve with pinto beans on the side. Makes 1 quart Chili.

NEW YORK CHILI

  4 pounds coarsely ground
    beef
  1 large onion, chopped
  2 cloves garlic, minced
  1 tablespoon cumin seed,
    ground

  2 tablespoons chili powder
  3 or 4 dashes hot pepper
    sauce
1-1/2 cups canned tomatoes
    Salt
  2 cups hot water

Lightly brown meat, onion and garlic in heavy skillet. Add cumin, chili powder, pepper sauce, tomatoes, salt to taste and hot water. Simmer 1 hour. Makes 2½ quarts Chili.

TEXAS CHILI

2 tablespoons cooking oil
3 pounds boneless chuck,
   cut in 1/4-inch cubes
3 or 4 cloves garlic, minced
6 tablespoons chili powder

2 teaspoons ground cumin
1 tablespoon oregano
3 tablespoons flour
2 quarts Beef Broth
   Salt and pepper

Heat oil in heavy skillet. Add beef, stirring until it loses its pink color. Lower heat and add garlic. Combine chili powder, cumin, oregano and flour. Sprinkle meat with mixture, stirring until well coated. Stir in Broth. Season to taste with salt and pepper. Bring to the simmering point, then reduce heat, cover and simmer 2 hours, stirring occasionally to keep meat from sticking. Add water if necessary. Serve with extra chili powder and a hot pepper sauce. Makes 1¹/₂ quarts Chili.

WYOMING CHILI

1 cup onions, thinly sliced
4 tablespoons green pepper,
   diced
3 tablespoons cooking oil
2 pounds beef, cut in 1/2-inch
   cubes
1 cup boiling water

1 cup tomato juice
3 tablespoons chili powder
1/4 cup cold water
2 teaspoons sugar
3 cloves garlic, minced
2 (No. 2) cans Kidney beans
   Salt

Cook onions and peppers in hot oil until tender. Add beef cubes. Cook uncovered until browned. Add boiling water, tomato juice and chili powder, which has been mixed to a paste with the cold water, sugar and garlic. Cover and simmer 1 hour, then uncover and cook 1¹/₂ hours longer. Twenty minutes before serving, add beans. Season to taste with salt. Makes 1¹/₂ quarts Chili.

And for good measure here's a bonus, a really good tasting all-vegetable chili:

VEGETARIAN CHILI

2 cups dried pinto beans	1/2 teaspoon dried oregano
5 cups cold water	2 tablespoons chili powder
1 medium onion, chopped	2 cups tomato juice
2 cloves garlic, minced	Salt and pepper
2 tablespoons cooking oil	Sourdough bread
1/4 teaspoon powdered cumin seed	Parmesan cheese, grated

Soak beans overnight in water to cover. Next morning, drain, then add 5 cups cold water. Bring to a boil, reduce heat and simmer, covered, until tender and thickened. In a skillet, sauté onion and garlic in hot oil until lightly browned. Add to beans. Add herbs and tomato juice and stir to mix well. Cover and simmer over low heat about $1^1/2$ hours, stirring occasionally. Season to taste with salt and pepper. Serve over thick slices of sourdough bread. Sprinkle servings with Parmesan cheese. Makes $1^1/2$ quarts Chili.

Chilled Soups

A crystal cup of cold jellied soup can do wonders for lagging appetites on a sultry day.

Make them the day before and refrigerate overnight. In very hot weather, chill the serving cups 2 or 3 hours beforehand in the refrigerator.

For an appetite-tempting hot weather meal, serve one of these chilled soups with dainty sandwiches and fresh fruit.

BORSHT

3 cups fresh beets, peeled and grated raw (by hand, in food chopper, or run quickly through blender)
2 quarts water

3 tablespoons lemon juice
1 tablespoon sugar
2 eggs, well beaten
    Salt and pepper
    Sour cream

Cook grated beets in water until tender-crisp. Add lemon juice and sugar. Cool. Blend eggs well with cooled beet mixture. Season to taste with salt and pepper. Garnish serving bowls with sour cream. Makes 2^1/$_2$ quarts Borsht.

ICED BEET SOUP

2 cups Brown Stock
2 cups clear beet juice (from
   canned or cooked beets)

2 tablespoons onion juice
1/2 cup red wine
   Cucumber slices

Combine Brown Stock and beet juice and heat to boiling. Add
the onion juice and blend well. Chill until icy cold. To serve,
add wine and pour over cucumber slices in each cup. Makes 1
quart Soup.

BUTTERMILK–CHICKEN SOUP

4 cups cultured buttermilk
1/2 medium cucumber, peeled
　　and chopped
1 cup cooked chicken, cut up

1 tablespoon celery leaves,
　　chopped
1 teaspoon prepared mustard
　　Salt and pepper
　　Fresh dill, chopped

Mix all ingredients thoroughly. Chill. Season to taste with salt and pepper. To serve, beat well and serve in chilled cups. Garnish each with chopped dill. Makes 1 quart Soup.

JELLIED BEEF SOUP

1 bay leaf
1 whole clove
1 teaspoon celery salt
1 teaspoon Worcestershire sauce
1 quart Brown Stock

　　Salt and pepper
2 teaspoons unflavored gelatin
1 tablespoon cold water
　　Sprig parsley

Add bay leaf, clove, celery salt and Worcestershire sauce to Brown Stock. Season to taste with salt and pepper. Heat to boiling and simmer 10 minutes over low heat. Meanwhile, in a cup, soften gelatin in the cold water. Add to hot broth mixture and stir well. Strain liquid through three thicknesses of cheesecloth and chill until firm. Garnish cups with chopped parsley. Makes 1 quart Soup.

CUCUMBER SOUP

2 large cucumbers, peeled and
  seeded, then chopped
1 small onion, chopped
3 tablespoons butter or
  margarine
1 quart Chicken Broth

Salt and pepper
1/2 cup milk
1/2 cup cream or evaporated
  milk
1 tablespoon fresh dill,
  chopped

Sauté cucumbers and onion in butter or margarine. Add broth and simmer 15 minutes. Force through a colander or food mill and season to taste with salt and pepper. Chill. To serve, add milk and cream or evaporated milk and blend well. Garnish cups with chopped dill. Makes 2 quarts Soup.

JELLIED TOMATO SOUP

1-3/4 cups water
    6 fresh tomatoes, chopped
    1 medium onion, chopped
    2 ribs celery, chopped
  1/2 green pepper, chopped
    1 tablespoon parsley,
      chopped

4 whole cloves
1 bay leaf
1 tablespoon unflavored
  gelatin
Salt and pepper

Add 1½ cup of the water to tomatoes, onion, celery, green pepper, parsley, cloves and bay leaf. Cover and simmer 20 minutes. Force through a colander or food mill. Meanwhile, in a cup, soften gelatin in remaining ¼ cup cold water. Add to tomato liquid, stirring until dissolved. Season to taste with salt and pepper. Chill until firm. To serve, arrange by spoonfuls in bouillon cups. Makes 1 quart Soup.

SORREL SOUP

6 leeks
1 small onion, chopped
6 tablespoons butter or margarine
3 stalks sorrel, chopped
6 cups Chicken Broth
3 small potatoes, sliced
1 clove garlic, minced

1/2 cup watercress, chopped
Sprig thyme
Sprig marjoram
Sprig parsley
1 cup cream or evaporated milk
Salt and pepper
1 tablespoon chives, chopped

Chop the white parts of leeks and mix with chopped onion. Sauté in butter or margarine until transparent but not browned. Add sorrel, Chicken Broth, potatoes, garlic, watercress, thyme, marjoram and parsley and simmer 45 minutes, stirring occasionally. Force through a colander or food mill. Add cream or evaporated milk. Season to taste with salt and pepper. Chill overnight. Garnish cups with chopped chives. Makes 1¹/₂ quarts Soup.

SPINACH BORSHT

1-1/2 pounds fresh spinach
1 quart water
1/4 cup sugar
1 tablespoon vinegar

2 tablespoons lemon juice
2 eggs, well beaten
1/2 cup sour cream
Salt and pepper

Wash spinach well. Remove stems and chop fine. Simmer in water 10 minutes. Stir in sugar, add vinegar and lemon juice and let cool. Mix beaten eggs and sour cream until well blended. Mix thoroughly with spinach mixture. Season to taste with salt and pepper. Serve very cold. Makes 1¹/₂ quarts Borsht.

VICHYSSOISE

4 large potatoes, chopped
2 small onions, chopped
3 cups Chicken Broth
2 tablespoons butter or
   margarine

2 cups milk
1 cup cream or evaporated milk
  Salt and pepper
  Minced chives

Simmer potatoes and onions in Chicken Broth until tender, about 20 minutes. Force through a colander or food mill. To the hot purée add butter or margarine, milk, cream or evaporated milk, salt and pepper to taste. Chill. Serve in cups garnished with minced chives. Makes $1^1/2$ quarts Vichyssoise.

WATERCRESS SOUP

2 cups watercress, chopped
3 cups Chicken Broth
4 tablespoons chicken fat
3 tablespoons flour

1 cup milk
1/3 cup cream or evaporated
   milk
   Salt and pepper

Simmer watercress in broth 20 minutes. Meanwhile, in another saucepan, melt chicken fat and blend in the flour. Gradually add milk and cook, stirring constantly, until smooth. Add to watercress broth and cook until thickened. Add cream or evaporated milk and season to taste with salt and pepper. Chill overnight before serving. Makes 1 quart Soup.

Fruit and Sweet Soups

Fruit soups are delicately-flavored, not-too-sweet purées of fruit which are slightly thickened and served in cups.

Serve fruit soup as an appetizer for dinner or with a light luncheon. Serve it warm or chilled, never hot.

APPLE SOUP

1-1/2 pounds tart apples
2-1/2 quarts water
   1 3-inch stick cinnamon
    Peel of 1/2 lemon
   5 tablespoons cornstarch
   1 tablespoon cold water

6 tablespoons dry white
  wine
  Sugar
1/2 cup heavy cream or
  evaporated milk, whipped

Wash apples. Do not peel, but cut in quarters and cut out cores. Cook until soft in 1 quart of the water with cinnamon and lemon peel. Force through a colander or food mill. Add remaining $1^1/_2$ quarts water and re-heat. Mix the cornstarch with 1 tablespoon cold water and stir into soup. Cook 5 minutes, stirring constantly. Remove from heat. Add wine and sugar to taste. Serve warm or chilled, garnished with whipped cream or evaporated milk. Makes $2^1/_2$ quarts Soup.

BERRY SOUP

2 cups berries (raspberries,
  blackberries, blueberries)
3-1/2 cups water
2 cups apple juice
Dash nutmeg
Sugar

2 tablespoons cornstarch
2 tablespoons cold water
1/4 cup lemon juice
Sour or whipped cream or
  evaporated milk

Simmer berries in water 20 minutes. Strain. To this juice add
apple juice, nutmeg and sugar to taste. Dissolve cornstarch in
cold water and add to combined juices. Cook, stirring constantly, until smooth. Chill. Add lemon juice and serve in bowls
garnished with whipped cream or sour cream. Makes 1^{1}/$_{2}$
quarts Soup.

DRIED FRUIT SOUP

1/4 pound dried prunes
1/4 pound dried apricots
1/2 cup dried apples
1/4 cup dried currants
1/4 cup raisins
2 quarts cold water

1/4 cup tapioca
1 stick cinnamon
Dash salt
2 cups apple juice
2 tablespoons sugar
Grated rind of 1/2 lemon

Soak dried fruits overnight in the water. Do not drain. Add
tapioca and cinnamon stick. Cover and cook 1^{1}/$_{2}$ hours in soaking water. Cool slightly and force through a colander or food
mill. Add salt, apple juice, sugar and lemon rind. Chill. Serve
very cold. Makes 2 quarts Soup.

SOUR CHERRY SOUP

1-1/2 cups sugar	2 tablespoons cornstarch
2 cups water	4 cups milk
1 quart fresh sour cherries, pitted	Salt

Add sugar and water to cherries. Cook over low heat 20 minutes, until cherries are soft. Force through a colander or food mill. Moisten cornstarch with a small amount of the milk, then add to hot cherry pulp. Cook, stirring constantly, until smooth and thickened. Add remaining milk and chill. Serve cold. Season to taste with salt, if desired. Makes 2 quarts Soup.

COCONUT SOUP

    2 cups coconut, grated   1/4 cup cold water
2-1/2 quarts water   1/4 teaspoon salt
  1/2 cup cornstarch   Sugar

Simmer coconut in water 1 hour over low heat. Strain. Dissolve
cornstarch in the cold water and add to coconut liquid. Cook,
stirring constantly, over low heat until thickened. Add salt and
sugar to taste. Makes 2 quarts Soup.

PUMPKIN SOUP

    3 cups raw pumpkin, cubed   1/4 teaspoon ground
    1 tablespoon sugar   cinnamon
1-1/2 cups water   Dash of nutmeg
    3 cups milk   3 tablespoons butter or
       Salt   margarine

Cook the pumpkin and sugar in the water until tender, adding
more water, if necessary, to keep from sticking. Force through
a colander or food mill. Heat milk to scalding, add the pumpkin
pulp and re-heat. Season to taste with salt, cinnamon and nutmeg. Add butter or margarine. Serve hot or warm. Makes $1^1/2$
quarts Soup.

PRUNE SOUP

  1/2 cup sugar   1/4 cup cornstarch
       Grated peel of 1/2 lemon   3 cups milk
    6 cups water   Salt
2-1/2 cups dried prunes

Add sugar, lemon peel and water to prunes and cook until very soft. Force through a colander or food mill. Moisten cornstarch with small amount of the milk and add. Add remaining milk and combine with prune pulp. Cook, stirring constantly, until slightly thickened. Season to taste with salt. Serve warm or cold. Makes 2 quarts Soup.

WINE SOUP

1 tablespoon cornstarch	2 cups boiling water
4 tablespoons sugar	2 slices lemon
1/8 teaspoon salt	2 cups dry white wine
Dash nutmeg	3 egg whites
3 egg yolks, beaten	1 tablespoon sugar

Combine the cornstarch with the sugar, salt and nutmeg, then blend with egg yolks. Gradually add the boiling water, stirring constantly. Add lemon slices and simmer over low heat 3 to 4 minutes. Add wine and heat but do not bring to a boil. Meanwhile, beat egg whites until stiff. Fold 1 tablespoon sugar into them. Drop spoonfuls of the beaten egg white on top of the hot soup. Cover tightly 3 minutes so the steam from the soup cooks the egg whites slightly. Pour into soup bowls with an island of egg white on top of each serving. Makes 1 quart Soup.

Stews

A hearty, thick version of soup, stew can be made of almost any combination of meats and vegetables, braised or simmered. The concentrated broth is thickened for gravy.

A good stew is almost a meal in itself. For a balanced meal, serve in bowls or plates with a tossed salad, a bread and a light dessert.

BAVARIAN STEW

2 pounds lean beef chuck, cut in 1-inch cubes	Salt and pepper
2 tablespoons cooking oil	3 tablespoons flour
2 cups water	1-1/2 cups flour
3/4 cup vinegar	3 teaspoons baking powder
3 large onions, sliced	3/4 teaspoon salt
1/2 teaspoon powdered cloves	2 tablespoons oil
	3/4 cup milk

Brown beef cubes in the cooking oil. Add water, vinegar and onions. Cover and simmer 2 hours. Add the cloves and salt and pepper to taste. Cook 20 minutes longer. Blend the flour with 2 or 3 tablespoons stew liquid, then add the paste to the stew. Cook, stirring constantly, until thickened. Sift together the 1½ cups flour, baking powder and ¾ teaspoon salt. Add to the milk the 2 more tablespoons of oil and add, all at once, to dry ingredients, stirring quickly to form a soft dough. Drop batter by spoonfuls on top of simmering stew, placing each spoonful on a piece of meat. Cover tightly and cook over low heat 15 to 20 minutes, without lifting lid. Makes 1¹/₂ quarts stew.

BEEF STEW

4 tablespoons flour	4 whole small potatoes,
1-1/2 teaspoons salt	peeled
1/8 teaspoon pepper	1/2 pound green beans
3 tablespoons cooking oil	(preferably fresh), cut in
1-1/2 pounds lean beef chuck,	1-inch pieces
cut in 1-1/2-inch cubes	Sprig parsley
3 cups water	1 bay leaf
1 tablespoon Worcestershire	1/2 teaspoon celery seed
sauce	Salt and pepper
2 medium onions, quartered	3 tablespoons flour
6 small carrots, cut in	1/2 cup cold water
3-inch pieces	

Combine 4 tablespoons flour, 1¹/₂ teaspoons salt and ¹/₈ teaspoon pepper. Meanwhile heat cooking oil in large iron skillet or Dutch oven. Dredge beef cubes in flour mixture and brown in hot fat. Add the water and Worcestershire sauce and cover. Simmer over low heat 1 hour, or until meat is tender. Add onions, carrots, potatoes, green beans, parsley, bay leaf, celery seed and more water, if necessary. Simmer 30 minutes longer, or until vegetables are tender but not too soft. Remove parsley and bay leaf and season to taste with salt and pepper. Blend 3 tablespoons flour and ¹/₂ cup water to make a thin paste. Slowly pour enough of this into stew, stirring constantly, to thicken it slightly. Makes 1 quart Stew.

BRUNSWICK STEW

1 stewing chicken, cut up	2 medium tomatoes, chopped
1 medium onion, chopped	2 cups cooked lima beans
2 quarts water	1 cup fresh corn (preferred)
Salt and pepper	1 cup fresh okra (preferred)
1/4 teaspoon dried thyme	2 tablespoons flour
1 bay leaf	2 tablespoons cold water

Simmer chicken and onion in water over low heat 2 to 3 hours, until tender. Remove chicken from broth and chill broth to congeal fat. Lift off hardened fat. Meanwhile, remove chicken from bones and cut meat in bite-size pieces. Season broth to taste with salt and pepper, then add back chicken pieces. Add thyme, bay leaf, tomatoes, lima beans, corn and okra. Simmer another 30 minutes. (Note: If canned whole kernel corn or okra are used, cook only 15 minutes.) Remove bay leaf. Combine

2 tablespoons flour and 2 tablespoons cold water to make a paste. Stir in enough paste to thicken stew slightly. Makes 1¹/₂ quarts Stew.

CHICKEN STEW

1 stewing chicken, cut up	1/2 cup water
2 tablespoons oil	2 cups flour
1 medium onion, chopped	4 teaspoons baking powder
1 clove garlic, minced	1 teaspoon salt
2 cups tomato juice	3 tablespoons parsley,
2 cups water	chopped
Salt and pepper	2 tablespoons oil
2 cups fresh or frozen peas	1 cup milk
3 tablespoons flour	

Sauté chicken in 2 tablespoons hot oil until golden brown. Add onion and garlic and cover. Cook 5 minutes over low heat. Add tomato juice and water. Cover and cook 2 to 3 hours, until chicken is tender. Remove chicken and cool. Chill broth to congeal fat, then lift off hardened fat. Pull meat from chicken bones and add—in large pieces—to the broth. Re-heat broth and season to taste with salt and pepper. Add peas and simmer 10 minutes. Meanwhile, blend the 3 tablespoons flour and ¹/₂ cup water to make a thin paste. Gradually stir in enough of this paste to thicken stew slightly. Make dumplings by combining 2 cups flour, 1 teaspoon salt, baking powder and parsley. In a measuring cup, combine milk and oil, then add all at once to flour mixture. Stir quickly with a fork to make a soft dough. Drop by spoonfuls into the boiling stew. Cover tightly and simmer 15 minutes without removing cover. Makes 1¹/₂ quarts Stew.

CHEESE STEW

2 cups leftover beef roast,
   cut in 1-inch cubes
1 cup raw potatoes, chopped
1 tablespoon onion, chopped
1 tablespoon green pepper,
   chopped
1 small carrot, chopped
3 tablespoons cabbage,
   chopped

3 tablespoons parsley,
   chopped
3 cups Brown Stock
   Salt and pepper
2 tablespoons flour
2 tablespoons cold water
1/2 cup grated American or
   cheddar cheese
   Paprika

Simmer beef, potatoes, onion, green pepper, carrot, cabbage
and parsley in Brown Stock 30 minutes, until vegetables are
tender. Season to taste with salt and pepper. Thicken slightly
with a paste made from the flour and cold water. Add cheese
and stir until cheese is melted. Garnish servings with paprika.
Makes 1 quart Stew. Note: Do not can this Stew.

CREOLE STEW

1 stewing chicken, cut up
2 quarts water
2 green peppers, chopped
1 medium onion, chopped
1/2 pound ham, cubed

1 quart fresh or canned
   tomatoes
   Salt and pepper
2 cups fresh or
   frozen peas

Simmer chicken in water 2 to 3 hours, until tender. Remove
chicken and chill broth to congeal fat, then lift off hardened fat.
Pull meat from chicken bones in large pieces and return meat
to broth. Add peppers, onion, ham and tomatoes. Cover and
simmer 1 hour. Season to taste with salt and pepper. Add peas
and cook 10 minutes longer. Makes 2 quarts Stew.

DANISH STEW

1/4 cup flour	2 tablespoons cooking oil
1 teaspoon salt	1/2 teaspoon sugar
1/8 teaspoon pepper	3 tablespoons lemon juice
1-1/2 pounds round steak, cut in 1-1/2-inch squares	3 cups hot water
1 small onion, sliced	4 medium potatoes
	Salt and pepper

Combine flour, 1 teaspoon salt and the pepper. Dredge steak squares in flour mixture and brown meat and onion in hot oil. Mix sugar and lemon juice and stir in. Simmer 3 to 4 minutes over low heat. Add hot water and cover. Simmer until meat is tender. Add peeled and cubed potatoes and cook until tender. Season to taste with salt and pepper. Makes 1^1/$_2$ quarts Stew.

HUNGARIAN STEW

3 tablespoons cooking oil	1 teaspoon caraway seed
4 tablespoons flour	1/2 teaspoon paprika
1 teaspoon salt	2 cups water
1/8 teaspoon pepper	2 pounds (3 cups) sauerkraut,
2 pounds lean beef, cut in	drained
1-1/2-inch cubes	Salt and pepper
1 medium onion, chopped	1 cup sour cream

Heat oil in heavy skillet. Combine flour, 1 teaspoon salt and $^1/_8$ teaspoon pepper. Dredge meat cubes in flour mixture and brown in hot oil. Add onion, caraway seed, paprika, water and sauerkraut. Cover and cook over low heat until meat is tender. Season to taste with salt and pepper. Just before serving, add sour cream. Makes 2 quarts Stew. Note: Do not can this stew.

IRISH STEW

2 pounds uncooked corned beef	2 turnips, sliced
6 peppercorns	2 carrots, sliced
2 blades (or 1 tsp. ground) mace	1 onion, sliced
1 teaspoon celery seed	2 tablespoons vinegar
Sprig parsley	3 tablespoons flour
Sprig marjoram	2 tablespoons water
2 quarts water	Salt and pepper
2 potatoes, sliced	

Place beef, peppercorns, mace, celery seed, parsley and marjoram in stew kettle. Add water and cover. Simmer 45 minutes. Strain broth and taste. If very salty, dilute or discard and replace with 2 quarts boiling water. Return beef and simmer $1^1/_2$ hours longer, until meat is tender. Cut meat into 2 or 3-inch pieces and return to broth. Add potatoes, turnips, carrots and onion. Cover and simmer 30 minutes, until vegetables are tender. Combine flour with vinegar and 2 tablespoons water to make a thin paste. Stir into stew to thicken. Season to taste with salt and pepper. Makes 1¹/₂ quarts Stew.

DUTCH STEW

2 tablespoons cooking oil	2 quarts water
1/4 cup flour	1 tablespoon Worcestershire
1 teaspoon salt	sauce
1/8 teaspoon pepper	1/4 cup flour
1/2 pound lean beef, cut in 1-inch cubes	1/4 cup cold water
	Salt and pepper
1/2 pound lean pork, cut in 1-inch cubes	1-1/2 cups flour
	1 teaspoon salt
1/2 pound beef liver, cut in 1-inch cubes	3 teaspoons baking powder
	3/4 cup milk
2 small onions, sliced	1/4 cup cooking oil

Heat 2 tablespoons oil in heavy skillet. Combine ¹/₄ cup flour, 1 teaspoon salt and ¹/₈ teaspoon pepper and dredge cubes of all three meats in mixture. Brown in the hot oil. Add onion and stir 5 minutes while it cooks. Add water and Worcestershire sauce. Cover and cook over low heat 1¹/₂ hours, or until meats are tender. In a cup, blend ¹/₄ cup flour and ¹/₄ cup cold water to make a thin paste. Add to simmering stew and stir until smooth and thickened. Season to taste with salt and pepper.

Make dumplings by combining 1¹/₂ cups flour, 1 teaspoon salt and baking powder in a mixing bowl. Mix ¹/₄ cup oil and milk in a measuring cup and add, all at once, stirring briskly to make a soft dough. Drop dough by spoonfuls into simmering stew. Cover tightly and simmer 10 minutes. Makes 1¹/₂ quarts Stew.

KIDNEY STEW

2 small kidneys
2 cups cold water
1 tablespoon lemon juice
1 1/2 teaspoons salt
2 cups boiling water
6 bacon slices
1/3 cup flour

1/8 teaspoon pepper
3 tablespoons onion, chopped
Salt and pepper
1 tablespoon parsley, chopped
2 cups hot cooked rice

Wash kidneys. Split and remove membrane, fatty core and veins. Rinse well. Cut into 1/2-inch cubes. Cover with 2 cups cold water mixed with lemon juice and 1/2 teaspoon of the salt. Soak 30 minutes. Drain and rinse in cold tap water. Simmer 30 minutes in 2 cups boiling water. Lift out kidneys and reserve cooking liquid. Drain kidney pieces on paper towel. Fry bacon slices until crisp. Drain, saving fat. In a bowl, combine flour, remaining 1 teaspoon salt and 1/8 teaspoon pepper. Dredge cooked kidney pieces in seasoned flour and brown in hot bacon fat. Add onion and brown in fat. Crumble bacon slices and add. Stir in flour left over from dredging. Add 2 cups liquid in which kidneys were cooked. Cook, stirring constantly, until thickened. Season to taste with salt and pepper and garnish with chopped parsley. Serve over hot rice. Makes 1 quart Stew.

OVEN STEW

2 pounds lamb, cut in 1-inch cubes
2 tablespoons cooking oil
1 medium onion, sliced
2 cups water
1 tablespoon Worcestershire sauce

2 tablespoons flour
2 tablespoons cold water
Salt and pepper
1 cup fresh or frozen peas
3 medium carrots, sliced
1 rib celery, sliced

Brown meat in hot oil in Dutch oven or heavy skillet with lid. Add onion and cook, stirring, 5 minutes. Add water and Worcestershire sauce. Cover pan and bake 1^1/$_2$ hours in 325-degree oven. Blend the flour with 2 tablespoons cold water and add, stirring to blend in well. Season to taste with salt and pepper. Add peas, carrots, and celery and bake 30 minutes longer. Makes 1^1/$_2$ quarts Stew.

LAMB STEW

1/4 cup flour	1 tablespoon Kitchen
2 teaspoons salt	Bouquet
1/4 teaspoon pepper	3 cups water
2-1/2 pounds lean lamb, cut in	1 bay leaf
1-1/2-inch cubes	1 teaspoon dried thyme
1/4 cup cooking oil	4 medium potatoes, peeled
12 small whole onions	and quartered
12 whole fresh or canned	6 medium carrots, cut in
button mushrooms	3-inch pieces
1 clove garlic, minced	3 tablespoons flour
1 teaspoon sugar	1/2 cup water
2 sprigs parsley	Salt and pepper
1 tablespoon Worcestershire	
sauce	

Combine flour, salt and pepper and dredge lamb cubes in mixture. Heat oil in large iron skillet. Brown lamb over medium heat. Remove meat and add onions, whole mushrooms, garlic and sugar to skillet. Sauté 5 minutes, stirring frequently. Return lamb to skillet and add parsley, Worcestershire sauce, Kitchen Bouquet and water. Cover, lower heat and simmer 30 minutes. Add bay leaf, thyme, potatoes and carrots and cook 45 minutes longer. Meanwhile, blend 3 tablespoons flour with ^{1}/$_2$ cup water and gradually add to stew, stirring constantly. Cook 10 minutes longer. Remove parsley sprigs and bay leaf and season to taste with salt and pepper. Makes 2 quarts Stew.

MULLIGATAWNY STEW

2 tablespoons butter or
  cooking oil
1/4 cup minced onion
1/4 cup cooked ham, chopped
1 blade (or 1/2 tsp. ground)
  mace
3 whole cloves
1 teaspoon curry powder
1 teaspoon parsley, chopped
6 cups Chicken Broth

1/2 cup cooked diced chicken
1/3 cup celery, chopped
2 cups cooked or canned
  tomatoes
1/2 cup raw apple, chopped
  Salt, pepper, cayenne
1 tablespoon tomato catsup
1 cup cooked rice
1 lemon, sliced

Sauté onion and ham in butter or oil until onion is transparent. Tie mace, cloves, curry and parsley in a piece of cheesecloth and put into soup kettle. Add broth, chicken, ham and onion mixture, celery, tomato and apple. Cover and cook over low heat 1 hour, or until vegetables are tender and flavors are mingled. Remove spice bag and discard. Season soup to taste with salt, pepper and cayenne. Add catsup. Serve over cooked rice and garnished with lemon slices. Makes 2 quarts Stew.

RABBIT STEW

2 cups dried lima beans
1 rabbit, cut up
3 cups water
1 bay leaf
1 medium onion, chopped
6 carrots, sliced

1 green pepper, chopped
2 tablespoons butter or
  margarine
2 tablespoons flour
  Salt and pepper

Simmer beans and rabbit pieces in water 2 hours. Add bay leaf and onion and cook 30 minutes longer. Remove bay leaf and add carrots and green pepper. Simmer 30 minutes longer, adding more water if needed. In another saucepan, melt butter or margarine and blend in flour. Gradually add to it 1 cup cooking broth and cook, stirring, until thickened. Add back to stew. Season to taste with salt and pepper. Makes 1¹/₂ quarts Stew.

SQUIRREL STEW

1 squirrel, cut up	2 tablespoons cooking oil
2 cups water	1 small onion, chopped
1/2 cup vinegar	1 rib celery, chopped
1 teaspoon mixed pickling spices	2 medium onions, quartered
	6 carrots, cut in 3-inch pieces
1/4 cup flour	Salt and pepper
1 teaspoon salt	2 tablespoons flour
1/8 teaspoon pepper	2 tablespoons cold water

Soak squirrel 2 to 3 hours in water, vinegar and pickling spices. Remove and dry meat. Reserve liquid. Dredge in mixture of ¹/₄ cup flour, 1 teaspoon salt and ¹/₈ teaspoon pepper. Brown pieces in hot oil. Meanwhile, heat water in which meat soaked to boiling. Simmer 10 minutes and strain, pouring liquid over meat and discarding spices. Add chopped onion and celery and cover. Simmer over low heat 1¹/₂ to 2 hours, or until tender. Add quartered onions and carrots and cook 30 minutes more, until vegetables are tender. Season to taste with salt and pepper. Combine 2 tablespoons flour and 2 tablespoons cold water and add, stirring until thickened. Makes 1 quart Stew.

TOMATO BEEF STEW

2 tablespoons cooking oil
2 tablespoons flour
1 teaspoon salt
1/4 teaspoon pepper
2 pounds lean beef, cut in
   1-1/2-inch cubes
4 cups tomato juice

6 small whole onions
6 small whole carrots
6 small whole potatoes
2 tablespoons flour
2 tablespoons cold water
  Salt and pepper

Heat oil in large iron skillet or Dutch oven. Combine 2 tablespoons flour, 1 teaspoon salt and $^1/_4$ teaspoon pepper. Dredge meat cubes in flour mixture and brown in hot oil. Add tomato juice, cover and simmer over low heat 2 hours, or until meat is tender. Add onions, carrots and potatoes and cook 45 minutes. Blend 2 tablespoons flour and 2 tablespoons cold water to make a thin paste. Add to stew and stir until thickened. Season to taste with salt and pepper. Makes 2 quarts Stew.

SPANISH STEW

2 pounds lamb, cut in
   1-1/2-inch cubes
2 tablespoons cooking oil
2 quarts hot water
1 medium onion, chopped
1 green pepper, chopped
1/2 cup uncooked rice

3 medium tomatoes, peeled
  and quartered
  Salt and pepper
1 egg, beaten
1 teaspoon cooking oil
1/2 teaspoon vinegar

Brown lamb cubes in hot oil until golden brown. Add water and cover. Simmer over low heat $1^1/_2$ hours. Add onion, green pepper, rice and tomatoes and cook 30 minutes longer. Season to taste with salt and pepper. Combine egg, oil and vinegar and add. Stir until thickened. Makes $1^1/_2$ quarts Stew.

VENISON STEW

2 pounds venison, cut in 1-1/2 to 2-inch cubes	2 medium carrots, sliced
1/4 cup flour	1/2 cup celery, chopped
1 teaspoon salt	1 medium onion, sliced
1/4 teaspoon pepper	2 tablespoons flour
2 tablespoons cooking oil	2 tablespoons cold water
2 cups water	1 tablespoon lemon juice
	Salt and pepper

Coat meat cubes with ¹/₄ cup flour to which 1 teaspoon salt and ¹/₄ teaspoon pepper have been added. Brown in hot oil. Add water, cover and cook over low heat 1¹/₂ to 2 hours, until tender. Add carrots, celery and onion and cook 15 minutes longer. Blend 2 tablespoons flour with 2 tablespoons water to make a thin paste. Add to stew and stir well until thickened. Add lemon juice and season to taste with salt and pepper. Makes 1¹/₂ quarts Stew.

Garnishes and Accompaniments to Serve With Soup

A bright garnish or a crunchy accompaniment can turn a ho-hum soup into a gourmet dish.

By appealing to the senses of sight, taste and texture, the soup cook can add variety and interest to any meal without adding appreciably to the cost or time. Most garnishes can be created in minutes from ingredients already on hand.

Select a garnish as carefully as you would the dishes in a menu. The right one can add crunch to a smooth soup, a dash of color to a white soup, or exciting flavor to a bland soup.

Sprinkle small amounts of the following on bowls or tureens of soup to add contrast in color, taste, or texture:

For Color:

Grated cheese; chopped unpeeled red apples; dollops of catsup or chili sauce; sliced or chopped hard-cooked eggs; thin slices of lemon (including rind); a dash of ground nutmeg or cloves; diced uncooked red or green bell peppers; chopped fresh parsley; thinly sliced stuffed olives; sliced red radishes; sour or whipped cream sprinkled with paprika; shredded cooked carrots.

For Texture:

Crisp dry cereal; toasted chopped nuts; crisp-fried bacon pieces; salt pork cracklings; broken corn chips; popcorn; broken potato chips; canned French fried onion rings; chow mein noodles; cracker crumbs; grated raw carrot or turnip.

For Flavor:

Grated lemon or orange rind; sliced wieners; sautéed mushrooms; chopped chives; Parmesan cheese; chopped cucumber; chopped mint; crushed dried celery leaves; flaked canned fish; crumbled fried hamburger; sautéed chopped onion.

The following garnishes and accompaniments will add special interest to your homemade soups:

ALMOND BALLS

24 almonds	2 egg whites
1/2 cup bread crumbs	Hot oil for deep-fat frying
1/2 teaspoon salt	

Blanch the almonds and chop or grind fine. Mix with the bread crumbs, salt and just enough egg white to bind together. Work with the hands to form tiny balls. Roll in remaining egg white, then drop quickly, a few at a time, into hot oil. Fry until golden brown and drain.

BREAD CRISPS

Cut bread slices in long, narrow strips and dip in melted butter or margarine. Brown in 300-degree oven.

CHEESE BALLS

1/4 cup butter or margarine	3/4 cup flour
1/2 cup cold water	3 eggs, unbeaten
1/4 teaspoon salt	1/2 cup grated cheese
Dash cayenne	(any type)
1/8 teaspoon paprika	Hot oil for deep-fat frying

Melt butter or margarine. Add water and cook 2 minutes. Stir in seasonings and flour and cook, stirring, until mixture will form a dough. Cool slightly, add eggs, one at a time. Add cheese and drop from a teaspoon into hot oil. Fry until golden brown. Drain.

CHEESE PUFF BALLS

1/4 cup grated cheddar cheese	1 egg white
4 tablespoons flour	3 tablespoons dry bread
1/2 teaspoon grated onion	crumbs or cracker crumbs
1/4 teaspoon salt	Hot oil for frying
Dash cayenne	

Blend the cheese, flour, onion, salt, cayenne and stiffly beaten egg white. Shape into small balls and roll in crumbs. Fry until golden brown, about 2 minutes in the hot oil. Drain.

CHEESE CRACKERS

Spread packaged soda crackers (or homemade crackers: pages 163-165) thinly with butter or margarine. Cover tops with grated cheese. Toast in 350-degree oven 5 minutes, until cheese melts and is lightly browned.

CHEESE STRAWS

1-1/2 cups flour	4 tablespoons ice water
1/2 teaspoon salt	1 cup grated process cheese
6 tablespoons shortening	

Mix flour and salt. Cut in shortening until mixture is granular in appearance. Stirring with a fork, work in just enough ice water to form a stiff but workable dough. Roll out very thin on a floured board. Spread one half the dough with grated cheese and top with the other half of the dough. Fold over and roll out. Repeat. Cut into 3 by $^{1}/_{2}$-inch strips. Bake on cookie sheet in 450-degree oven until golden brown.

CHICKEN LIVER BALLS

1/4 pound chicken livers	Salt and pepper
2 tablespoons melted butter or margarine	4 egg yolks
	4 tablespoons fine bread crumbs
1/2 teaspoon parsley, finely chopped	Hot oil for frying

Sauté livers in butter or margarine. Force through a colander or food mill. Add parsley, salt and pepper and enough of egg yolks to make a smooth, workable material. Form into small balls, then roll in bread crumbs and fry in hot fat. Drain.

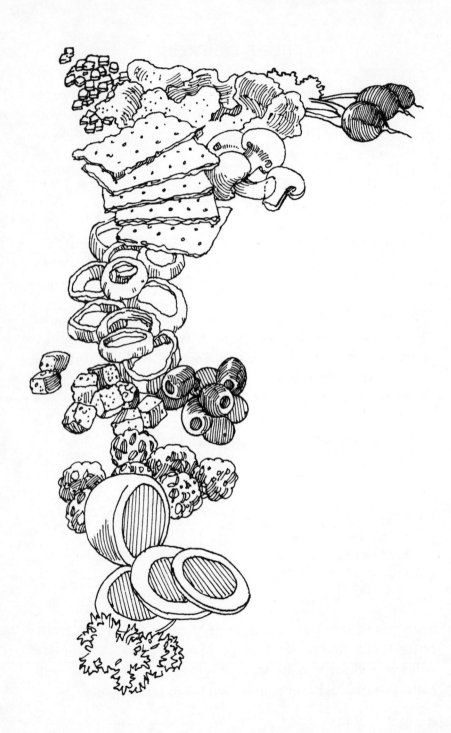

CHICKEN QUENELLES

1/2 pound cooked chicken meat	1 egg, slightly beaten
2 tablespoons soft bread crumbs	1/2 teaspoon salt
2 tablespoons milk	2 cups Chicken Broth heated to boiling
2 tablespoons butter or margarine, melted	

Grind chicken meat through fine blade of food grinder. Soak bread crumbs in milk, then force through colander or food mill. Add butter, egg, chicken meat, salt and enough of the bread-crumb-milk mixture to make a workable consistency. Shape with two spoons and drop into boiling Chicken Broth. Cook until firm.

CHESTNUTS IN CONSOMMÉ

24 chestnuts, shelled and blanched	2 quarts Consommé

Drop chestnuts into boiling Consommé and simmer until just tender, about 10 minutes.

WHEAT CRACKERS

3 cups flour	1 cup butter or margarine
1/2 teaspoon salt	1 cup creamed cottage cheese

Combine flour and salt. Using two knives, the hands or a pastry blender, cut in butter or margarine and cottage cheese until well blended. Work into a dough. Wrap in waxed paper and chill at least 1 hour. Roll out 1/8-inch thick on a well-floured board. Cut into round, square or fancy shapes with a knife or a cookie cutter. Place on ungreased baking sheet. Pierce each cracker several times with a fork. Bake in a 450-degree oven 12 to 15 minutes, until lightly browned. Cool on rack.

WHOLE WHEAT CRACKERS

Use whole wheat flour (or one half whole wheat and one half white flour) in the Wheat Crackers recipe.

CARAWAY CRACKERS

Add 4 teaspoons caraway seed to the cracker dough.

SESAME-ONION CRACKERS

Add 4 teaspoons sesame seeds and 4 teaspoons grated onion to cracker dough.

POPPY SEED CRACKERS

Top crackers with poppy seeds before baking.

HERB CRACKERS

Add 4 teaspoons chopped chives, 4 teaspoons chopped parsley or 4 teaspoons chopped dill to the dough before rolling out.

CORNMEAL CRACKERS

1 cup yellow cornmeal	1/4 teaspoon Tabasco sauce
1-1/2 teaspoons sugar	1-1/2 cups boiling water
1 teaspoon salt	1 egg white
1 teaspoon grated onion	
2 tablespoons butter or margarine	

Combine cornmeal, sugar, salt, onion, butter or margarine and Tabasco. Add boiling water and stir until water is absorbed. Stir in slightly beaten egg white. Drop by teaspoonsful on greased baking sheet. Bake 15 minutes in 400-degree oven. Cool on rack.

CROUTONS

Croutons may be made fresh easily and quickly just before serving soup. For variety and good nutrition, use whole wheat, rye or cracked wheat breads occasionally.

PLAIN CROUTONS

Remove crusts from day-old bread slices. Cut into cubes and toast in 250-degree oven 15 minutes, or until golden brown.

CHEESE CROUTONS

Cut crusts from whole wheat bread slices. Butter slices, then cut into cubes. Sprinkle with grated cheese and broil 2 or 3 minutes until cheese melts and becomes golden brown.

GARLIC CROUTONS

Blend ⅛ teaspoon garlic salt in 2 tablespoons butter or margarine. Spread over bread slices. Cut into cubes and broil 2 to 3 minutes, until golden brown.

EGG BALLS

4 hard-cooked eggs
1 teaspoon salt
1 egg yolk
1 egg white, slightly beaten

2 tablespoons flour
2 cups any seasoned broth,
   heated to boiling

Shell the eggs and cut in half. Remove the yolks. Reserve the whites for use in sandwiches or salads. Mash the yolks smoothly. Add salt and enough of the raw egg yolk to make a workable dough. Shape into tiny balls and dip in egg white, then in flour. Drop, a few at a time, in boiling broth and lower heat. Simmer 5 minutes and drain.

EGG CUBES

1 egg yolk
1/2 cup soft fresh bread crumbs
1/4 teaspoon salt

1 tablespoon butter or
   margarine, softened
Hot oil for frying

Mix the egg yolk, crumbs, salt and butter or margarine. Work with a spoon to a smooth mixture. Scrape onto a greased sheet of waxed paper and cover with another sheet of waxed paper. Pat or roll to ½-inch thickness. Remove top paper and cut dough in ½-inch cubes. Fry in hot oil 1 to 2 minutes. Drain.

FARINA PUFFS

2 tablespoons butter or margarine	1 egg yolk
3 tablespoons uncooked farina (or Cream of Wheat)	1/8 teaspoon salt
1/2 teaspoon baking powder	2 cups Beef Broth heated to boiling

Cream butter or margarine and blend in farina and baking powder. Add well-beaten egg yolk and salt. Drop by ¹/₄ teaspoonfuls into simmering Broth. Cook 10 minutes, until doubled or tripled in size.

MEAT DUMPLINGS

3/4 pound cooked beef	1-1/2 teaspoons baking powder
2 sautéed chicken livers	1/8 teaspoon salt
1 onion, sliced and sautéed	1 egg, slightly beaten
1 egg	1/4 cup chicken fat, melted
Salt and pepper	1/4 cup water (about)
1-1/2 cups flour	

Grind beef, livers and sautéed onion through fine blade of food chopper. Add the egg and season to taste with salt and pepper. In another bowl, combine flour, baking powder, ¹/₈ teaspoon salt, the other egg and chicken fat. Blend well, then add enough water to make a soft dough. Roll out about ¹/₈-inch thick and cut with a biscuit cutter. Place a teaspoon of the meat mixture in the middle of each round and fold dough over to form a half moon. Pinch edges together to seal. Pierce the tops of dumplings with a fork, place on a greased baking sheet and bake 20 to 30 minutes in a 400-degree oven.

FORCEMEAT BALLS

4 tablespoons finely chopped
   cooked meat (from making
   soup stock)
4 tablespoons bread crumbs
1/2 teaspoon salt
   Dash of pepper

1 teaspoon parsley, chopped
1/2 teaspoon onion juice
1 egg yolk
2 quarts seasoned broth,
   heated to boiling

Combine chopped meat with bread crumbs. Season with salt, pepper, chopped parsley and onion juice. Add enough egg yolk to make mixture workable. Blend well and form into marble-size balls. Drop into gently simmering broth. Cook 5 minutes. Lift out and place in soup bowls. Pour hot broth over them.

OYSTER FORCEMEAT BALLS

1/2 cup shelled oysters
   Oyster liquor
1/2 cup fresh mushrooms
1 tablespoon butter or
   margarine

1/2 cup bread crumbs
   Salt
1 egg yolk

Parboil oysters 3 to 4 minutes in their own liquor. Chop. Sauté mushrooms in butter or margarine. Chop and add to oysters. Add bread crumbs, salt to taste and enough egg yolk to form a workable mixture. Roll into small balls. Put on a small greased baking sheet and bake 5 minutes in a 350-degree oven.

MARROW BALLS

1/2 cup soft bread crumbs	Dash of pepper
1/4 cup cooked bone marrow, chopped	1 egg yolk
	1 egg white
1/2 teaspoon salt	2 quarts Consommé
1/2 teaspoon onion juice	or seasoned broth

Combine bread crumbs and marrow. Add salt, onion juice and pepper. Mix well, then gradually add egg yolk to make a workable consistency. Roll into marble-size balls. Beat egg white slightly. Quickly dip balls into egg white, then drop into boiling consommé or broth. They will first drop to the bottom, then rise to the surface. As soon as they float (about 2 minutes), lift out. Place in soup bowls or tureen and pour hot broth over them.

MATZO BALLS

2 egg yolks	1/2 teaspoon salt
3 tablespoons chicken fat, melted	2 egg whites
	2 quarts hot Chicken Broth
3/4 cup matzo meal	heated to simmering
1/2 cup hot Chicken Broth	

Beat egg yolks into chicken fat until well blended. Add matzo meal, 1/4 cup at a time, alternately with the 1/2 cup of hot broth. Add salt and chill 1 hour. Form into small balls, adding more matzo meal if necessary. Chill balls 3 hours. Roll in beaten egg whites and drop, a few at a time, into simmering Broth. Simmer 15 to 20 minutes. Serve in Chicken Broth.

MIXED VEGETABLE CUBES

1/2 cup puréed leftover mixed
     vegetables
  2 egg yolks
  1 whole egg

1/2 teaspoon salt
     Dash of cayenne
1/2 cup Brown Stock, or White
     Stock heated to boiling

Purée vegetables by running through a blender or forcing
through a colander or food mill. Combine egg yolks, whole
egg, vegetables, salt and cayenne. Blend well. Add hot stock
and pour 1 inch deep into buttered shallow pan. Set in a pan
of hot water and bake in 300-degree oven 35 to 45 minutes,
until set. Cut into cubes. Place cubes in soup bowls and pour
broth over them.

RICE BALLS

  1 cup cold cooked rice
  2 tablespoons flour
  1 egg
1/2 teaspoon salt

     Dash nutmeg
  1 teaspoon grated lemon rind
  2 cups Chicken Broth
     heated to boiling

Force rice through a colander or food mill. Add flour, egg and
seasonings. Roll into small balls and drop into boiling Broth.
Simmer 5 minutes.

FRITTERS

  1 egg, beaten until foamy
  1 tablespoon water
  1 tablespoon lemon juice

1/2 cup flour
1/2 teaspoon salt
     Hot oil for deep-fat frying

Beat egg with the water and lemon juice. Blend in flour and salt. A spoonful at a time, pour the batter through a colander directly into the hot oil. Fry 1 or 2 minutes or until golden.

PEA BLOCKS

1 cup cooked or canned peas	2 egg whites
1/2 teaspoon salt	2 quarts Consommé
Dash of pepper	or any seasoned broth
1 teaspoon celery seed	

Drain peas and press through colander or food mill. Blend in salt, pepper, celery seed and egg whites. Pour into a small greased baking pan and set in a pan of boiling water. Bake in 350-degree oven 45 minutes, or until set. Cut into blocks. Place blocks in soup bowls and pour hot Consommé or broth over them.

SPINACH BLOCKS

1 pound fresh spinach	1/2 teaspoon salt
1 egg, well beaten	1 quart Consommé or any
1 drop Tabasco sauce	seasoned broth

Wash spinach but do not drain. Chop fine, then cook over very low heat in only the water that clings to the leaves. Drain and force through a colander or food mill and add the egg, Tabasco and salt. Pour into a small greased baking pan and set in a pan of boiling water. Bake in 350-degree oven until set, about 30 minutes. Cut into blocks and place in soup bowls. Pour hot Consommé or broth over blocks.

TOMATO BLOCKS

1/2 cup thick tomato paste	2 egg whites, slightly beaten
1/2 teaspoon salt	2 quarts Consommé or
1 drop Tabasco sauce	seasoned broth

Paste may be canned or may be made by forcing cooked or canned tomatoes through a colander or food mill, then cooking the liquid down until thick. To $1/2$ cup paste, add salt, tabasco and egg whites. Pour into a small greased baking pan and set in a pan of boiling water. Bake in 350-degree oven 45 minutes, or until set. Cut into blocks and place in soup bowls. Pour hot Consommé over blocks.

WHIPPED CREAM

For White or Green Soups:

1/4 cup heavy cream, chilled	1 tablespoon tomato purée
1/8 teaspoon salt	

Beat cream until fluffy. Add salt and tomato purée and drop by spoonfuls on each serving of hot soup.

For Tomato Soups:

Omit tomato purée and add 1 tablespoon horseradish.

Index

Recipes are cross-indexed by main ingredients, which are printed in *italics*. See Contents for general types of soups.

Other Garden Way Books
You Will Enjoy

The Complete Guide to Growing Berries & Grapes, by Louise Riotte. 142 pages, quality paperback, $3.95; hardcover, $5.95. What to plant where, when, and exactly how.

Profitable Herb Growing at Home, by Betty E. M. Jacobs. 240 pages, quality paperback, $5.95. The perfect book for those who wish to expand a home herb garden into a money-making country sideline.

What Every Gardener Should Know About Earthworms, by Dr. Henry Hopp. 40 pages, quality paperback, $1.50. The benefits of earthworms in making richer soils and bigger crops.

Secrets of Companion Planting for Successful Gardening, by Louise Riotte. 226 pages, quality paperback, $4.95, hardcover, $8.95. For bigger, more luscious crops.

Down-to-Earth Vegetable Gardening Know-How, featuring Dick Raymond. 160 pages, deluxe illustrated paperback, $5.95. Special durable cover edition, $7.95. A treasury of complete vegetable gardening information.

Keeping the Harvest: Home Storage of Vegetables & Fruits, by Nancy Thurber and Gretchen Mead. 208 pages, deluxe illustrated paperback, $5.95; hardcover, $9.95. The very best of the food storage books.

Vegetable Gardening Handbook, by Roger Griffith. 120 pages, spiral bound, $3.95. Take it into your garden, for information and as your own record book.

Dwarf Fruit Trees for the Home Gardener, by Lawrence Southwick. 118 pages, quality paperback, $3.95; hardcover, $5.95. All you need to know to start a home orchard on a small plot.

Improving Garden Soil With Green Manures, by Dick Raymond and Richard Alther. 48 pages, 10 x 8. Paperback edition, $2.50. An illustrated, no-frills handbook that shows the tremendous difference green manures can make in improving your garden.

Let It Rot!, by Stu Campbell. 152 pages, quality paperback, $3.95. Homemade fertilizers for a healthier garden.

Cash from Your Garden, by David Lynch. 208 pages, 5½ x 8½, illustrated. Quality paperback $3.95. The book that tells how to turn your garden produce into extra income.

The Home Gardener's Cookbook, by Marjorie Blanchard. 192 pages, quality paperback, $4.95; hardcover, $6.95. Mouth-watering recipes using your garden produce.

Treasured Recipes from Early New England Kitchens, by Marjorie Blanchard. 144 pages, quality paperback, $4.95; hardcover $8.95. Yesterday's favorite recipes, adapted to today's kitchens.

Woodstove Cookery: At Home on the Range, by Jane Cooper. 204 pages, illustrated by Sherry Streeter, $5.95. A warm and friendly introduction to buying, installing, and cooking on a kitchen wood-burning range, with hundreds of time-tested recipes.

Homemade: 101 Easy-to-Make Things for Your Garden, Home, or Farm, by Ken Braren and Roger Griffith. 176 pages, deluxe illustrated paperback, $6.95. A wonderful collection of simple projects for the home carpenter.

These books are available at your bookstore, or may be ordered directly from Garden Way Publishing, Department SS, Charlotte, VT 05445. If order is less than $10, please add 60¢ postage and handling.